7 Pre-game Habits of Pro Hockey Players

Preparation Leads to Consistent On-Ice Success!

7 Pre-game Habits of Pro Hockey Players:
Preparation Leads to Consistent On-Ice Success

Published by Score100goals Publishing

For Information on the book or other Score100goals products address:

Score100goals
18 Coldbrook
Irvine, CA 92604

ISBN: 978-0-615-31264-4

Cover Design by: Leslie Sears and Brett Henning
Cover Photo by: Garrett Henning

www.Score100goals.com

Contents

FAQ—Doubter Read This

Can you become a better hockey player by mentally preparing yourself before a game? I think you know the answer to this question.

Here are some of the most common doubts, fears, and insecurities that players have before they commit themselves to a new pre-game routine.

Do I have to completely change my current game or learn some voodoo mind technique for a quick fix?

No on both accounts. There are specific techniques pros use in their pre-game routine from incorporating visualization for increasing your confidence to a number of different breathing techniques that help you stay focused. These will help you realize your full potential on the ice. How does a natural hothead condition himself to play within the frustrations of every game, yet continue to help his team on the ice without taking penalties? How do you remain focused as everything around you is falling apart? It's all here.

Do I have to play in the AHL, Europe, or NHL to see the benefits of preparing for a game?

Not at all. This book is for anyone willing to put in the extra time to improve their game. More and more players are starting from the earliest age to train with strength, conditioning, and power skating coaches to be the best physically conditioned athletes on the ice. This means players at the highest levels are within the same general physical fitness level. As Wayne Baughman, one of the greatest wrestling coach's ever said, "Mental preparation is the one thing that separates the Olympic athlete from just the good athlete. Very definitely, at the highest level of competition, the mental and emotional level is the most important aspect of winning, because the athletes are, or should be, fairly equal on a physical level." You must separate yourself by including the mental aspect that few players take into account.

If you're sick of seeing minimal results with you or your parents paying thousands of dollars for hockey camps, doing the same power skating and off-ice training as all the other players in your age group, then apply the techniques in this book before every game. I promise it will make you better.

Do I have to have a certain temperament or personality to play hockey?

Many people believe they can't control their temper and are destined to spend more minutes in the box than the coach may like. At the other end of the spectrum, some players have a laidback personality and think they can't develop that killer instinct or desire that makes good players great. This is completely untrue. According to David Krauss in the book *Peak Performance*

> A person's long-standing personality traits are less relevant to producing good athletic performance than are the individual states of mind, like anxiety or excitement, that the athlete can bring about at particular times for the purpose of readying.[1]

This book will teach you specific ways to control your emotions and how to get into the peak state needed for optimal performance.

Do I have to use the visualization or breathing techniques? I just want to have a better mental attitude going into every game.

NO. Those are just a couple of options outlined in the book. If you read and try to understand the principles and thinking behind each technique you will be more prepared going into each game. The more you know, the better you will play. If you actually practice some (or hopefully all) of these techniques/skills, I guarantee you will be better prepared, mentally and physically, for each game. This can only translate to becoming a better player. "Success leaves tracks." It's not a secret that every pro in any sport goes through specific mental exercises before every game. Growing up they learned from other players and maybe

---

[1] *Peak Performance: Mental Game Plans for Maximizing Your Peak Potential,* David R. Kauss, Prentice Hall, 1981.

even their parents, as Tiger Woods so famously did, that the mental aspect of the game is more important then the physical.

Do I need to have good grades, be book smart, or go to college to understand the principles?

Not at all. Every great personal success in every field of life uses some of these techniques. It's not a question of being smart. As I learned more and more about successful people, I began to see similarities in their mental attitudes. According to *How to Think Like Leonardo da Vinci: Seven Steps to Genius Everyday* by Michael Gelb they're 7 forms of intelligence that can be measured.[2] One of them is athleticism. And if you play hockey then I immediately give you the benefit of the doubt that you have a great control over the mind body interaction. Some of the techniques outlined in this book are things you may already do, and others are brand new. They may not come easily at first, but the exercises can be practiced just like the power play or penalty kill. As you get better and continue to focus on your mental preparation, this will propel your game to the highest level.

If I use some of the 7 steps outlined in the book before every game, will I see noticeable improvements?

Yes, I guarantee you improvements if you practice and implement these 7 techniques into your game day routine. (*You will learn how to develop a routine, if you don't currently have one.*) I know that you've been preached to about physical conditioning and overall mental attitude. These are the cornerstone of any great athlete. You have to have the mental attitude to break through obstacles. Basically, no great athlete in any sport gets there with talent alone. You can have all the tools coming into the game including talent, preparation, the will to win, peak physical conditioning, and the many other intangibles needed to play your best. But practicing these techniques will lift you to the next level even faster.

---

[2] *How to Think Like Leonardo da Vinci: Seven Steps to Genius Everyday*, Michael Gelb, Element Books, 2004

From the book *Mind Gym* "Sports psychology is the science of success. Studies show that within a group of athletes of equal ability, those who receive mental training outperform those who don't almost every time. Mental skills, like physical skills, need constant practice."[3]

[3] *Mind Gym*, Gary Mack and David Casstevens, McGraw- Hill, 2001

MY STORY AND WHY YOU NEED THIS BOOK

My captain cranked up the volume of Metallica's "One." It was now blaring out of the visitor's locker room.

The opening weekend of the college hockey season had finally come. Looking down the hallway at the other 25 players in the brand new Wisconsin rink, we were supposedly one of the best teams in the country. We traveled by bus from South Bend, Indiana, to play the inaugural game at the Kohl Center. The new home of the Wisconsin Badgers. For us, it was the culmination of getting out of bed at 6 a.m. for strength and conditioning training, then preseason practice, and now finally, the season was hours away.

"How's everyone feeling today? First game in the season, but this one means a lot, especially to the Minnesota boys," our captain, Brian, yelled out to us as he led the stretch.

"Great," I replied while joking with the rest of the guys, realizing at this moment that everyday in this environment was a dream come true.

"Are you nervous?" my buddy Sam, who was another freshman on the team, asked.

"I'm a little nervous. Feeling a few butterflies floating around in my stomach." I mean, how could you not be nervous, playing in front of a sold out rink with 18,000 fans for your first college game? There were a couple of doubts that kept running through my mind like a ticking time bomb. Could I hang with these guys? Would I be able to score? Would I take a stupid penalty? Or even worse, be the focus of tomorrow's video session making the mistake that costs us the game?

Those thoughts vanished, as quickly as they appeared, when I pulled the Notre Dame game jersey over my head for the first time in my college career and walked out of the runway to the deafening sound of boos. I stepped onto the ice in the middle of it all. Emotions were running through me like a Mac Truck. I was so pumped up that my hands were shaking and I was almost hyperventilating. Yet, I still had little doubts in the front of my mind.

I was playing hockey in front of 18,000 people and although there was definitely a smile plastered across my face, I was nervous as heck......................

Every kid growing up playing hockey fantasized about having their name on the back of the jersey of their favorite NHL team. We spent countless hours all winter playing hockey on ponds with cracks that could swallow your skate and then ball hockey all summer. I can't tell you how many tennis players I ticked off taking up three courts. But tough luck, right? Our sticks were bigger than their racquets and we were ready to offend even the cutest girl that threatened to interrupt our game. How many times have you heard your mom yelling threats at you to come home for dinner? That was me and my friends, as I'm sure it was or still is you too.

As we got older and moved our way up the hockey ladder, we eventually practiced more under better coaches. We spent our summers at week-long, overnight camps that seemed like a never ending crossover drill. Most players that reach the high levels follow generally the same path. Besides the few destined to play in the show since they were 5, most kids are pretty equal talent wise. The dedicated players climbing their way up the ladder are funneled into the same leagues and summer teams. This means the on-ice and off-ice training are very similar.

So how do you separate yourself from the pack?

How does an average player become great in a short time frame? This is what we call a late bloomer. Martin St. Louis, who was not drafted, led the league in scoring in 2004 and sipped from the Stanley Cup that same year. Lucky Luc Robitaille was drafted in the ninth round and ended his career with 668 Goals as a

Hollywood legacy. Or how about Henrik Zetterberg, who was drafted 210 overall in the 1999 draft, who is currently dominating the NHL. Surely the NHL scouts aren't that bad. I hope not, because my dad makes his living as one. The truth, at least the truth that I have come to know since my playing days have ended, is that a huge part of the game is mental. Ex-baseball player Frank Howard says "the trouble with professional sports is that by the time you learn how to play the game, you can't play anymore." What he means is that as a player you know so much more about the mental aspect of the game in the twilight of your career. This book will introduce you to mental development at an earlier age and give you that advantage. Learn from the mistakes of other players because you won't have time to make them all yourself.

Can you use these 7 steps alone and light the lamp in the NHL tomorrow?

Nope.

Can you use the 7 principles to greatly improve upon the physical skills you currently have and double your scoring tonight, cut defensive errors in half, and be relied upon in the final moments of a game?

I genuinely think you can.

"Contests for supremacy on the very highest levels are wages not physically, but mentally. When the very best boxers step into the ring to struggle for championships or when the finest martial artists square off, the contests will be determined, in most instances, by the mental edges of the winners."[4]

It helps to know where it all started for me. Strangely enough, it was on the tee box of a Southern California golf course. I have been playing golf about as long as I have been playing hockey. I still can't figure it out. I can crush the ball a

---

[4] *Toughest Men in Sports: Looking for the Mental Edge,* Mike Chapman, Culture House, 2001

mile, but your guess is as good as mine as to where it's going to end up. This hit me in the head like a brick right after I launched yet another golf ball into the houses along the 12th fairway. I waited in suspense hoping not to hear the sound of glass shattering. Solid thump! I was lucky this time. I wouldn't have to pony up the 500 bones or more that I didn't have to fix some rich retiree's window. At this point, in college, I would have launched my graphite driver Happy Gilmore style into the nearest tree. However this would/did completely ruin whatever game I had going. Fortunately this time I restrained myself because I was playing with the club pro Ken. Over the remaining holes, Ken (a jedi of self control) talked about visualizing your swing before stepping up to the tee. He told me it's a common routine that becomes automatic before every shot. He also taught me another way the pros controlled their emotions which was through breathing exercises. Smart guy-that Ken. Not only are the homeowners along the holes in the Southwestern United States safer, but I dropped my score and started the first step in applying these techniques into other areas of my life, including hockey. The best part about these techniques is that they can be instantly applied. You can shoot pucks into a tarp all summer and maybe score an extra 10 goals this season. You can also apply the book's following 7 techniques in conjunction with your practice to improve even more. I guarantee it.

THE IDEA BEHIND THIS BOOK

I have learned basic mental preparation techniques along the way but nothing was overall helpful to my game. Most people, my past self included, thought that eating a bunch of carbs, attempting to touch your toes once or twice, and listening to a pre-game talk by the coach was enough. There's more to it, as evidenced by the pre-game routine of every Pro Player in the NHL.

As mentioned before, in today's game there's little physical difference between most of the players. In the Toughest Men in Sports book, Mike Chapman writes about the 10 toughest dudes in the 20th century, including Muhammad Ali and Bruce Lee. He says this about their physical conditioning- ["all super athletes have been blessed with the physical necessities to become great. They have the required genes, which provide them with a base and the opportunity to rise to the very pinnacle of success. They have access, for the most part, to the same kinds of training facilities, teachers, methods, schools, and nutritional sources—at least in relative sense. Yet some excel- going on to become world and Olympic champions, while others are incapable. The difference, it seems safe to suggest, is mental. We can study it. We can observe instances of supreme mental conditioning and try to utilize what we learn."][5] This book will help you elevate your existing physical skills through mental preparation. You can use the techniques in this book to gain a mental advantage and separate yourself from other players. Whether your dream is to play in the NHL, become a better coach or more helpful parent, avoid injuries in a beer league, or even lower your handicap, this book will give you the mental tools needed to make it a reality.

What makes this book different?

First, I realize that in the past, any talk of mental preparation was most likely done by someone that didn't know much about hockey. A parent or even a psychologist would stand

---

[5] *Toughest Men in Sports: Looking for the Mental Edge,* Mike Chapman, Culture House, 2001

up in front of the team and try to explain the mental state needed to play at your best. I don't mean to casually dismiss their pep talks, but unfortunately I think many of you did. I've sat in the locker room or in one-on-one sessions as someone tried to explain how hockey is 90% mental and 10% physical. I agree now, but at the time my teammates and I were skeptical at best-just as you probably are right now. That's why I've tailored every exercise to hockey and got insight from pros that have played the game. What did they personally do before each game? What worked for them was adapted for the book and what didn't was left out.

Second, this book is not about getting results somewhere down the road. It's about adopting it as soon as possible and seeing results immediately. This is a fast paced society. If you don't see results in tonight's game, then it's forgotten and the techniques are lost. I want you to score more goals, come up with that big mid-ice hit or win that last minute face-off tonight.

Third, I'm not going to spend time on the problem. I'm going to assume that you show up to the rink, tape your stick, and get ready for warm-ups without mentally preparing for the game. This will give everyone an equal starting point. If you do mentally prepare, then you're already ahead of the game and this book will just add to your preparation. If you show up to every game expecting your physical skills to compensate for the lack of mental preparation then implementation of this book will improve your game even more.

Over the course of the book, I will explain 7 ways to help you get ready before every game. These 7 skills will give you a distinct advantage over other players. The steps and strategies can be used with incredible results---whether you are a player that's one step away from the pros or just playing for fun in a rec league. As a parent, you can teach your kids the techniques slowly and have them adopt them over the season. I learned from reading about Tiger Wood's childhood that it's never too early to focus on mental preparation. Just don't be psycho about it.

The pros in the 70's rarely skated in the summer, lived on

cheeseburgers and fries, and drank beers after the game. They didn't even know what an Olympic lift was. Now players work out like machines, have private chefs, and have their blood checked for missing minerals. Why not also increase the skills you have spent countless hours developing by mentally and physically preparing before every game? Just try the 7 following techniques. Get a good understanding of each technique by re-reading the chapters if you have to, then use it before the next game. It's a win-win situation. It can only make you a better player and it's easy to do. Try it and you're pre-game routine will change forever.
Here is the 7 step process you'll use to improve your game.

1. **Visualization**—First see and experience each game's most important plays in your mind before they happen. Of course, you don't know what's going to transpire in any given game, but using the 80/20 principle (explained in the Visualization chapter); you can pinpoint certain areas that will personally affect your game. This section breaks down visualization techniques which ultimately develops greater confidence. I give personal examples and show how this helps not only hockey players, but also other occupations such as golfers or doctors.
2. **Breathing**---is essential to life. Joking. But in all seriousness, how you breathe will not only enhance your mental clarity but also affect a number of other physical factors including your adrenaline level, blood oxygen level, muscle tightness, etc. These factors alone play a big part in your game but when out of control it's devastating. Breathing is a process rarely used and often ignored by amateur athletes. The book goes through specific exercises to do before a game and also in stressful situations such as overtime. From 4,000 year-old yoga breathing techniques to life or death big wave surfing breath preparation, you will learn how to manage your internal state through conscious breathing manipulation.
3. **Controlling Your Emotions**---Hockey is one of the most

intense sports in the world. We skate in a 185" by 85" enclosed space with ice as a floor, at breakneck speeds with 5 foot long sticks. A sport where players with a nasty streak---such as Chris Chelios---excel. There's a stat for how many times you physically hit someone and also one for fighting. Every player or parent reading this book has played in or seen a tough game. Coaches and announcers metaphorically compare it to a war. But with all this chaos going on out on the ice, the best players still control their emotions. We've all gone through or seen the ups and downs of a long season. A passion for the game is needed to compete at the highest level. But passion can easily spill over to stupidity and destroy a player. How can you stop emotions from negatively affecting your play? How can we suppress a negative emotion and turn it into a positive force? Do not let yourself be called a mental midget.

4. **Stretching**---I'm sure you go through a few stretching exercises, whether in the locker room, rink hallway or on the ice, before each practice and game. From my experience it's a quick drag of the leg for the hamstring, a couple of stick rotations for the wrist, and then you finish with a once up and down toe touch. This just isn't good enough to prepare your body for a hard hitting game that greatly taxes your body. In the book I give you a bunch of hockey specific dynamic stretches so you can pick and choose what's right for you. You will see the added benefits to your game from being properly stretched.
5. **Physical Warm-up (Games)** ---Every pro has individual physical warm-ups they use to get prepared for each game. Some run the stairs; others go off into a corner for a longer stretch, and some stick handle a golf ball with a weighted stick. It took me 15 years of playing hockey to realize that it's okay to approach a game with a less than serious attitude as every individual has their own individual peak state. The book highlights fun games such as team soccer, tennis ball games, stick-handling, and others that you can incorporate

into your pre-game warm-up. I will explain each technique and benefit that I personally know from experience or by speaking with pros themselves. Then the book shows you how to apply them into your warm-up for maximum benefit in tonight's game.

6. **Nutrition**---Many people, especially those growing up in the video game era, don't know the first thing about nutrition. (Opting for the fried chicken sandwich over the Big Mac isn't a good trade off.) I'm not going to insult your intelligence, but I will provide the fundamentals of proper game day nutrition. This knowledge is essential for your grocery shopping habits and then cooking meals for maximum performance. Hockey is a physical sport with 30 minutes of maximum intensity in a normal game. Eating the correct food, at the proper time in the proper ratios is critical. The book goes over specific foods that pros eat, and some other supplements they take to enhance performance. Some of the information is cutting edge food combinations and some are your standard favorites. The book explains what you should eat the night before a game, first thing in the morning, as a pre-game meal, snack, and post game. I only want to give you options, and then you take what works and discard what doesn't. Through trial and error you will find foods within a week that will give you that needed energy boost to reach the next level.
7. **Routines**---Every great player goes through a specific routine before each game and big plays, such as a penalty shot. In fact, if you analyze your pre-game routine, you will see patterns start to emerge. Every player either unconsciously or consciously does certain things before the game. However, some of these routines may be hurting you more than helping. The book looks at the mental benefits as well as internal changes you go through in a pre-game routine. Then we break down what you do now and how we can develop a routine that works for you.

***Personally, I don't believe I ever realized my full potential.*

*I was always stuck in my head, analyzing every little thing, which took me away from the present. More importantly I could've had a lot more fun playing a game I can only watch now because of an injury. I'm not going to sing you a Kenny Chesney song, but I would give up practically anything to be back on the ice for a number of games that I let slip away without being truly focused. My goal of this short book is to teach you 7 techniques that I know will help you achieve greater results on the ice. Whether you're an NHL player that could beat me in a race skating backwards, a 14-year old junior hockey player with the world in front of you, a recreational beer league player, or the parent of a 10 year old that thinks about hockey 24 hours a day, this book is for you.***

It's time to have fun and let the rest follow.

BRETT HENNING
Newport Beach, California
November 11, 2007

*I originally intended this book to be for everyone playing the game of hockey that could appreciate the mental aspect of the game---from 14 year old bantams to men's league players--- as a quick way to get better. But then while reading different books, articles, and other information as background before writing this book I realized that a great majority of superstar athletes developed a positive mental attitude at an early age. Most mentioned how Tiger Wood's dad enlisted a psychologist friend to help his mental toughness.

This led me to focus also on parents of hockey players. You spend the money and travel every weekend to sit in the cold stands and watch them play. I know that you would do anything to help them succeed. Mental preparation is often a neglected aspect of hockey that you can instill in them that will push them forward. Without being overbearing, I feel parents can help their kids mentally master the game from a young age- just as Tiger's dad has proved.

Chronology of Humbleness

"I've made a life long study in psychology, because it's in the mind where you separate the winners from the losers," said Hayden Fry, a college football coach for 37 years and recently inducted into the College Football Hall of Fame.

This book teaches 7 principles that pro players use in every sport to maximize individual skills and consistently deliver greatness. In between weekends of hops-inspired fun in my early 20's, I immersed myself in self-improvement material. A little bit of a contradiction- but for some reason, I enjoyed learning about the way people think and act. Everyone is different, but if you're reading this book then we all have the common backbone of early morning practices in cold rinks. I really believe that what I've learned since the end of my hockey career can help you in yours. My hockey background is the following:

- Moved to Canada from Long Island, NY when I was 15 to play Junior hockey with the Cambridge Winterhawks in the Mid-Western Junior B league
- That summer I was selected to the USA national Under-17 year old team and traveled to Verimaaku, Finland for exhibition games against Sweden and Finland
- Member of the Inaugural USA Under-18 team in Ann Arbor, MI
- Played college hockey at the University of Notre Dame
- Played on the USA team in the 2000 World Junior Championship in Skeleftea, Sweden
- Drafted by the New York Islanders
- Career ending injury when I severely herniated 2 discs in my neck

Unfortunately I didn't have any of the information in this book while I was playing.

How I even figured out this subject is a lesson in humility.

Fall 2002: After graduating from Notre Dame, I decided to use what little money I saved to book a one-way ticket to Australia and work/travel for a year. I wanted to get as far away from hockey (because of an injury I could no longer play) as I could and maybe learn to surf. I lived in a crowded hostel room with a bunch of Canadians. So much for getting away from hockey. All they talked about was hockey and as for surfing I nearly got my face rearranged by a group of territorial surfers, much like everyone's favorite actor Keanu Reeves in the movie Point Break. So it goes. However I did learn the preparation techniques of a former pro surfer staying at the same hostel. It was during a huge storm that whipped up 20 foot waves. In keeping with Keanu, it wasn't exactly the fifty year storm, but it was still literally a life and death situation. I watched the steps he went through to prepare for these massive waves. He lived through it, and I bought him a beer to figure out his secrets.

Spring 2003: I was staying in a small beach hostel in Byron Bay, Australia when the greatest season in pro sports started- HOCKEY PLAYOFFS. I missed hockey a lot, and when the Ducks began their Cinderella run I booked a ticket home. My Dad was an assistant coach for the team, and I had a free ticket to every game. Perfect. I watched every home game. But since I didn't have money for a plane ticket I was going to be forced to watch Game 7 of the Stanley Cup Finals on a 25" apartment T.V. As luck would have it the Ducks owner chartered a plane for the players' wives, and they had an extra seat. All the chips fell into place to see Game 7. I ended up sitting next to a top model that you see on TV all the time who was a friend of one of the player's girlfriends. I was literally so nervous by her looks that the only things I could stutter out of my mouth on a six hour plane ride were, "Where are you from?" and "What do you do?" *Smooth as Sandpaper.* Completely dejected I then sat through the Ducks' loss, while I beat the bag out of my inner self. I had to get a completely different game handled.

Winter 2003: After doing some research on the internet concerning girls, I found a "bootcamp" in San Francisco run by of all things an ex-hockey playing Canadian. They bring you out to bars and explain how easy it is to approach stunning girls. Thought I might give it a try. Couldn't hurt, right? This guy was a complete ninja with beautiful girl after beautiful girl. The interesting thing was the cutting edge psychological techniques that the instructors used to mentally prepare before going out. Needless to say, I became very interested in visualization, routines, anchoring, and many other things he talked about.

Summer 2006 I got back into hockey big time, playing 2 nights a week with a bunch of great ex-college, junior and pro hockey players. The hockey was great and I was mixing it up again with cool, like-minded people. I enjoyed every minute of it. It's very easy to meet new friends when you're on a team and a decent player. I got invited to play tournaments in Vegas and joined a league with a bunch of Hollywood actors. Then out of nowhere, in a one-month period I went from being one of the better players on the ice to the absolute worst. No joke. My teammates were yelling at me to catch a pass and pulling me aside after the game to question my commitment. Pretty weird for a beer league, but I guess that's hockey. Turns out my injury sustained during college 4 years ago was acting up again. The C-3 and C-4 discs in my neck were herniated and severely traumatizing my spinal cord. I needed surgery ASAP. For that ten-day period before surgery, while going through a battery of tests, I went into a mental tailspin. It became very clear to me at that point that your mental attitude affects not only your physical state, but your entire outlook on life. And for many of you, including myself, hockey was everything.

It's tough and rather stupid to analyze every move you made in the past but it brought me to one big conclusion- how you feel is how you play. Period. I knew that everything I learned from people way smarter than me could be translated to hockey. So I did my best to put it all together for you to learn from in the following pages.

Visualization

Visualization

I realize that "visualization" is a word that hockey players are quick to resist. They associate it with hypnosis and affirmations, but consider this……

- ***Jack Nicklaus***, considered by many to be the best golfer of all-time, winner of 18 Master Championships, visualized every shot before taking it. In his book *Golf My Way,* Nicklaus writes about the imagery he uses before hitting every shot. "It's like a color movie. First I 'see' the ball where I want it to finish, nice and white and sitting up high on the bright-green grass. Then the scene quickly changes and I 'see' the ball going there; it's path, trajectory, and shape, even its behavior on landing. Then there is sort of a fadeout, and the next scene shows me making the kind of swing that will turn the previous image into a reality…." [6]

- ***Arnold Schwarzenegger***, five time Mr. Universe, four-time Mr. Olympia has used visualization not only for athletic success but also credits it for his success as a movie star: "When I was very young, I visualized myself being and having what it was I wanted. Mentally I never had any doubts about it. The mind is really so incredible. Before I won my first Mr. Universe title, I walked around the tournament like I owned it. The title was already mine. I had won it so many times in my mind that there was no doubt I would win it."(Watch the movie Pumping Iron. During college this was my roommates favorite movie. In the movie Arnold tells Lou Ferrigno's parents, his main competitor and the man you know as the original Hulk, that he already called his mom and told her he won 5 days

[6] *Golf My Way*, Jack Nicklaus and Ken Bowden, Simon & Schuster, 1998

before the tournament even began. The guy is so cocky it's comical.)

- ***Nolan Ryan***, all-time leader in strikeouts and no hitters pitched, says "The night before a game I lie down, close my eyes, relax my body, and prepare myself for the game. I go through the entire lineup of the other team, one batter at a time. I visualize exactly how I am going to pitch to each hitter and I see and feel myself throwing exactly the pitches that I want to throw. Before I ever begin to warm up at the ballpark, I've faced all of the opposition's hitters four times and I've gotten my body ready for exactly what it is I want to do."

- ***Alex Rodriguez***, future Hall of Famer on the baseball diamond talks about visualization in the introduction to the book *Mind Gym*. "I can't tell you where I would be now if I hadn't seen myself wearing a big-league uniform long before it happened. Early in the 1996 season, I visualized winning the American League MVP award and holding it above my head. I visioned winning the batting title and holding up that trophy, too. I visioned a .380 batting average. In my mind I could see the number, flashing and blinking on exit signs......380...380...380."[7]

- ***Pele***, regarded as the greatest soccer player ever, would find a quiet place where no one would bother him to go through his visualization routine. An hour before every game he would lay on his back with a rolled up towel under his head and one placed over his eyes. He would then go through a mental movie of his soccer life. The mental movie started with him playing on the beaches of Brazil as a kid. It ended with him reliving the crowning moments of his career at the World Cup. He would bring

[7] *Mind Gym*, Gary Mach and David Casstevens, McGraw- Hill, 2001

the fun of playing as a kid and that winning feeling during his World Cup games to mind so he could use these feelings to fuel his fire for the upcoming game.

The list could go on and on. The truth of the matter is that in examining NASA astronauts, Olympic level athletes, Fortune 500 CEO's, neurologists, Special Forces Soldiers, musicians, and any field of considerable challenge, all the best use this technique to improve their performance. In the sports world they're called leaders (think Mark Messier) and in the business world they are called visionaries (think Steve Jobs of APPLE). They see it. They feel it. They experience it before they actually do it. They begin with the end in mind.

STILL DON'T BELIEVE ME. LET ME PROVE IT TO YOU ON A PERSONAL LEVEL

(Read over the next couple of paragraphs very slowly. Really feel the words described.)

Picture yourself relaxing around a table with good friends after a long day on the golf course or your favorite lake. Your good buddy just fired up the bbq and slapped 2 huge New York T-bones on the grill. He dumped all your favorite spices on it. With your favorite beverage in your hand, you sit back and take in the unbelievable smell smoking off the grill as the meat sears. He flips the steak once and all the juices from the top of the steak make the fire come up around it. Once again the smell hits you and stays with you for the next 7 minutes as you patiently wait for the come and get it call. Then he slaps the steak on your plate. The steak lands on your plate, steaming, with the juices pooling around it. You cut through it, stick the fork in it and put it in your mouth. Imagine chewing that first piece very slowly.

Anyone who is even half a fan of food as me will be salivating and even chewing that imaginary piece of steak. Or if that didn't phase you---you're not a man, but that's another story---another vivid example that we've all experienced is the startling wake up from a nightmare with your heart beating a million mph. Both of these above examples have no basis in reality, yet they elicit physical responses in your body. These are physical responses to something occuring solely in your mind.

How many times has every pro hockey player lifted the cup over his head before getting the chance to do so in real life? 5,10, 100, or most likely everyday since they were 5.

I'm going to organize this chapter by first giving a little background on visualization. This includes what you're trying to achieve as you practice it. There are fascinating, proven benefits from visualization. They concern both mental preparedness and also internal physical changes shown to improve performance. Secondly, I will walk you through the process of making "mind movies"-a catchphrase that signifies a personal visualization you can immediately use tonight to improve your play. As funny as it may sound, "mind movies" will make you a better player without a doubt.

Background on Visualization

Morpheus: Have you ever had a dream, Neo, that you were so sure was real? What if you were unable to wake up from that dream? How would you know the difference between the dream world and the real world?

Morpheus: If real is what you can feel, smell, taste and see, then 'real' is simply electrical signals interpreted by your brain— From the mind bending movie "The Matrix" (1999), and yes I realize this is another Keanu Reeves movie.

"Winners say, Of course I can do it! I've practiced mentally a thousand times. Losers, say, How can you expect me to do it? I don't know how!"
--Dennis Waitley

"Ninety percent of the game is half mental"
--Yogi Berra

Visualization is known by many names including guided imagery, mental rehearsal, mind movies, zoning in, and many more. I prefer my surfer buddy from Australia, who refers to it as "chilling out and letting his mind rip." The basic premise is the same for all of them- To see yourself positively completing or reliving a scene only in the mind. It's been proven to mentally raise a player's confindence, decrease anxiety and fear, and physically improve one's performance in the specific visualized area. Your brain literally cannot tell the difference between reality and a vivid mental thought/feeling. Visualization has been used since the beginning of recorded human history---yoga is over 4,000 years old--- and has been studied in a more in-depth manner since 1894 when Dr. Carpenter first studied the technique. I won't bore you with information from hundreds of positive studies in every walk of life. The bottom line as stated before is that if you take any group of overachievers you will see them consistently using visualization.

When and Where Visualization Has Been Used

A famous study clearly shows the benefits of visualization. The study was carried out at Wayne State University, Detroit, Michigan by one L. Verdelle Clark. He took three groups of basketball players and tested their ability to make free throws. He instructed the first group to spend twenty minutes a day physically practicing free throws. He told the second group (the control group) not to practice and had the third group spend twenty minutes a day only visualizing that they were shooting perfect basket after perfect basket. As might be expected, the control group that did nothing showed no improvement. The first group physically shooting baskets improved 24 percent, but through the power of imagery alone, the third group improved an astonishing 23 percent (this number is open to question and many believe it to be as high as 38 percent.)[8] This study has been tested in other sports such as downhill skiing, archery, and with the military for snipers. It's not a matter of testing to see if it works, because it undoubtedly does, but rather testing to see if there's any limit for mental and physical improvement using visualization.

The most common form of visualization is seeing yourself completing a specific task in the future. We're going to use it for hockey by visualizing scoring goals, making the big save, winning the last second face-off, etc. But before you stop and think that you can't, won't, and have never visualized, think about your daily habits. Everyday you wake up and see yourself driving to work, talking with your spouse, cooking/eating that night's meal, thinking about what movie you want to see, that cute member of the opposite sex that you keep trying to get the nerve to ask out, before they happen. How else would you accomplish anything if you didn't see yourself at least starting the task first? **The problem with nearly all people though is they imagine themselves in negative scenarios or at least limit**

---

[8] Clark, L.V. Effect of mental practice on the development of a certain motor skill. *Research Quarterly*. 31: pp 560-69, 1960

themselves to average achievements. Limits begin where vision ends. Visualization can then be a painful, debilitating everday process that holds you back without you every really realizing it. When these negative thoughts are focused on hockey it will severely hurt your game. You have to see yourself as a no-limit person. So therefore we want to use visualization techniques of pro players to improve your physical skills. But for someone with little to no experience in using positive visualization, how can you take a fluid game like hockey and pick out specific things to use? The following sidebar is a rule that can be applied not only to your hockey game but in all areas of your life.

80/20 rule

This is a common rule that applies to nearly everything in life. Founded by Vilfredo Pareto---a long dead famous economist and sociologist from Italy--- who noticed that 20% of his peapods he planted produced 80 percent of the peas. But not only did this apply to my man Vilfredo's peas, it also proved true in almost every area of life. This applies to a very long list of everyday activities and the ratio is often more like 90/10, 95/5, or even 99/1. What this means for hockey is that:

- 20% of a goalie's movements are responsible for stopping 80% of the shots.
- 20% of the defenseman's actions stop 80% of the opposing teams offensive rushes.
- 20% of a forward's actions account for 80% of his goals.
- 20% of a team's players score 80% of a team's goals.
- 20% of a teams' players takes 80% of a team's penalties.
- 20% of a team's players eat 80% of the post-game pizza and so on.

This means that you can analyze your game and break down the 20% of your on-ice actions that produce 80% of your desired results. NOW you have the 20% actions that make the biggest impact as a visualization starting point. What many don't realize- that successful people have recognized and figured out- is that you work hard to strengthen what you do best and simply keep a baseline of skills that you are inherently weak at.[9] What I mean by this is that if you have great speed but you're not a big hitter, then visualize and work on beating D wide, backchecking with speed, crashing the net for a rebound, and so on. Don't visualize open ice hits even though you want to be the next Dion Phaneuf. This may be against what you've heard time and again in the past (I think Vince Lombardi might even be on the other side of this statement) but think about it. When you work on your strengths or what you do best, then you multiple your results. If you work on fixing weaknesses then you get incrementally better. (try to Youtube Gretzky fighting or hitting and you don't get many results. Youtube him scoring and it's pages long.)

First start by looking at your past 10 games. Pick out the positive moments that jump out at you. From big game-winning goals down to small plays every coach loves and can make a difference in the game's outcome. Forget about the negative thoughts and breakdowns in your game. We will deal with eliminating these later in the chapter. Some positive examples are:

Forwards---

1. battling in front of the net for a rebound goal
2. chipping the puck off the boards and taking a big hit to get the puck out of the zone
3. driving the puck wide with speed and cutting to the net
4. a successful backcheck
5. great defensive positioning
6. great decisions 5 feet inside and outside the blueline

[9] The 4- Hour Workweek, Timothy Ferriss, Crown Publishers

7. finding a open spot in the offensive zone for a goal or tip.

Use these above examples as a reference point. Add some of your own and make them crystal clear, so you can really feel it as we will see later on in the chapter when we practice visualizing.

Defenseman---

1. a blocked shot
2. a tape–to-tape breakout pass
3. rushing the puck up the ice
4. clearing the front of the net
5. controlling the puck on the powerplay
6. one-timing a puck from the blueline
7. getting the puck to the net through bodies
8. rushing back to get the puck for a breakout.

Again use these as a reference point and add your own.

Goalies---

1. rebound control
2. glove save
3. blocker save
4. hugging the post on a wraparound
5. staying focused late in the game
6. looking around screens to make the save
7. moving post to post
8. having great angles
9. playing the puck around the net.

Create a clear mental picture of 10 positive plays of at least 10 seconds in length. Then jot these down on a piece of paper. (Take the time to do this. If you just read through this chapter then your game won't benefit. Don't be a lazy bum.) Just write the play simply- such as rebound goal against Team B. As long as you can take a quick glance at each written statement and immediately flashback in your mind to that play, it will have the desired effect. Then go over each play 3 quick times. Imagine your mind to be a Tivo. Play the movie once in fast forward, then in slow motion, and finally in real time. Now you have 10 10-second mind movies that you can refer back to as we go over how to actually visualize.

How to Visualize

"I went into a cocoon for 15-20 minutes before each game. This was my quiet time, my preparation time. I focused on the pitcher and how he would try to get me out. I would envision getting a hit off the pitcher."
---Wade Boggs, one of the greatest hitters ever in baseball

The most important aspect of visualizing is that you have to actually feel the experience in all of your relevant senses:

Sight---see yourself clearly on the ice, including the other team, your teammates, and fans in the stands
Sound---get juiced by the volume of the crowd, hear your skates cut through the ice, and the foghorn after a goal.
Touch---Feel the stick in your hand as you stickhandle, the force of a big hit, pushing through long strides
Smell---the distinct rink smell, breathing the cold air, that horrible glove smell

This may seem a bit odd at first, but the more intense and real the feeling, the greater the impression created on the brain. From a scientific perspective every experience in your life creates a new pathway in your brain. You can create this pathway through a physical experience or by simply thinking and feeling the same thoughts through visualization. The "mind movies" repeatedly emphasize your strengths which creates confidence through positive reinforcement. I can't teach you to hypnotize yourself so you can toe drag entire teams or shoot 100 mph, but visualization will generate confidence and give you expereince that you wouldn't otherwise gain. As you step onto the ice you have the feeling that you've been there before, and this experience (even though it's only mental) creates confidence. And remember the more vividly you recreate the experience you want to happen, the deeper and more permanent the pathway created will be. Keep this in mind through each exercise. ***OK, LET'S GET STARTED.***

Before you get to the rink, there's a certain amount of free time (bus ride to the rink, after pregame meal, etc.) When I was playing I would grab a couple of buddies to walk around the lobby of the hotel, check out the magazines/candy of the hotel lobby store(fat kid at heart), or walk around the block. Basically anything to waste the hours before the puck drops. The waiting was always the worst. I just wanted to play.

Instead of wishing this time away, you can use it productively by practicing visualization. It will effectively pass the time and make the game come quicker, but more importantly it will make you a better player. First, find a quiet place to go for the longest of the visualization techniques. At this time you can use the relaxation method and actually go through the entire visualization process described below. To learn the process I used a standard stock example meant for beginners that holds your hand and walks you through everything. It involves three steps with different options in each step. Go through each option exactly as shown below only a couple times at first. Figure out which one feels right so you can use it specifically next time. After the example below the book runs through different ways to tailor this for your own specific game.

Step 1: Relaxing your body and mind

"An anxious mind cannot exist in a relaxed body.....When one is anxious, so is the other. When one is at rest, so is the other."---Bernardo Leonard, a MLB batting Coach.

Everyone has had the experience of getting so fired up

that their face turns red, your muscles tense up, and your mind has one single thought which is usually violent in nature. The same way that you can generate these emotions that make you tense, you can also use your body to calm down and relax. It may seem counterintuitive but tensing your muscles even more and holding them in this position will bring you into a relaxed state upon release. Once you make your body relax the mind will follow and vice versa.

Option A

Sit or lay down in a comfortable position away from any distractions. This option involves physically tensing your muscles, holding the position for 5 seconds, then releasing. In between each step take two deep breaths. Don't rush through the steps. The goal is to relax with the process, not to race through it in the quickest time.

1. Start at your toes. Tense the toes by curling them. Hold for 5 seconds then release.
2. **TAKE 2 DEEP BREATHS**
3. Next tense your calf muscles. Hold for 5 seconds and release.
4. **TAKE 2 DEEP BREATHS**
5. Then tense your thighs by straightening your leg while flexing. Hold for 5 seconds and release.
6. **TAKE 2 DEEP BREATHS**
7. Tense your abdominal muscles by crunching your stomach. Hold for 5 seconds and release.
8. **TAKE 2 DEEP BREATHS**
9. Curl your fingers into a fist and hold for 5 seconds. Release.
10. **TAKE 2 DEEP BREATHS**
11. Tense your biceps as if you were starting to curl a weight. Hold for 5 seconds then release.
12. **TAKE 2 DEEP BREATHS**
13. Tense your shoulders by moving your elbows out and up so the arm is parallel to the ground at shoulder height. Hold

for 5 seconds then release.

14. **TAKE 2 DEEP BREATHS**
15. The final hold is your entire body. Tense everything you can for 5 seconds then release.
16. **TAKE 5 DEEP BREATHS**

This whole process should take around 3-5 minutes and leaves you relaxed for the visualization phase. Try **Option A** a couple of times after using the below two relaxation options. Weigh it against Option B and Option C. Decide which option puts you in the optimal relaxed state for the visualization sequence. Now you can repeatedly use this favorite option and discard the others. Or you can use them in conjunction with each other. Whatever gets the results you want.

Option B

Sit or laydown in a comfortable position away from any distractions. This option involves breathing in a regular pattern that relaxes the body. In a later chapter the book goes into more depth on the physical pluses of breathing and many different ways of practicing it, but for now this basic pattern will help relax you.

1. Start by taking a deep breath, inhaling through your nostrils for 4 seconds. It's important to actually feel your lungs fill with air and have your stomach rise.
2. Then hold your breath for 8 seconds. Feel your entire body relaxing.
3. Finally exhale for a total of 16 seconds. Feel the air emptying from the bottom of your lungs all the way to the top until there's no more air in your lungs. Your stomach will crunch in toward your spine as you exhale.

REPEAT THESE STEPS 5 TIMES

The inhale/hold/exhale ratio is 1:2:4. You can start with 4 seconds as the initial inhalation time and as you grow accustomed to it, you will need to increase this to 5,6,or even 7 seconds. After completing the breathing pattern 5 times, which will take also about 3-5 minutes then you will be ready to start the visualization phase.

Try **Option B** a couple of times to get relaxed before the visualization process. Weigh it against Option A and Option C. Which option gives you the best results? Now you can repeatedly use the best option for you and discard the others. Or you can use them in conjunction with each other. Whatever gets the results you want.

Option C

I used this when I was playing before I knew it's benefits. You may too. Sit or laydown in a comfortable position away from any distractions. Grab your iPod and put on your favorite slower song(s). For an example, I use (and don't judge):

- Dave Mathews Band
- Segur Ros
- some Led Zeppelin
- Pink Floyd
- James Taylor
- Theme music to *Gladiator*
- O.A.R.
- Bob Marley

It doesn't matter what song as long as it puts you in a relaxed mood. After listening for 5-10 minutes you will be ready for the visualization step.

Try **Option C** a couple of times. Weigh it against Option A and Option B. Which option gives you the best results for getting in a relaxed state? As stated above, take your favorite of the 3 options and use it while discarding the others. Or you can use them in conjunction with each other. Whatever gets the results you want.

Step 2: Visualize

This is where you vividly experience the 10 "mind movies" created before. Since visualizing is something new (and your mind hates anything new) your mind will try to trick you into simply not trying it. At this point in time, myself included, your mind persuades you that you can't think in pictures. Or you think this is dumb or not going to be beneficial to your game. Or it appeals to your ego and tells you how stupid you will look visualizing. Everyone's brain is adverse to change and work. (Kind of like in school when you had that term paper or big test and didn't start writing/studying until the night before. I've been there multiple times. Procrastination is a killer.) So do yourself a favor and stick with it. This may feel like a difficult process for some, but remember that all your thoughts are just quick snapshots of what you've previously experienced or been taught. For example when I say Ferrari, immediately a picture of a nice red car pops into your head. Then if you follow your thoughts, the next picture may be the car racing down the road at break neck speeds with you in the driver's seat, or the attention you would get, or the huge amount of cash you would have to fork over every month to own one/fix that nice red car. All of these thoughts are mental pictures strung together. So you really can think in pictures(visualize) and therefore create mind movies. It's even easier with the 10 mind movies you already wrote down, because you have either personally experienced them in the past couple of months or watched a player, on TV or live, do it. You have a baseline. Now it's a matter of experiencing these plays again in your mind with the same emotions as you originally felt. Just as the example of Jack Nicklaus, the golfer, at the beginning of the chapter where he could smell the cut grass in the air and feel the humidity during his visualization on the course, you also have to feel it with all of your senses. The stronger the emotions created and felt during the "mind movie," the more powerful of an effect it will have. Really try to imagine everything you would physically feel with all of your senses and also how you would emotionally feel during the play(confidence, enthiusasm, happiness, etc.) For a reference point on how to create your own "mind movie," I will walk you through one of my own. Notice the details I create and then apply it to each of your own mind movies. All the mind movies that you produce will be positive plays. Therefore you should feel an immediate sense of confidence as soon as you start visualizing the first one. This will continue to build through the entire visualization exercise. I played center, so my mind movie focuses on cycling down low, hitting an open linemate in the slot, then driving to the net for a rebound goal.

MY PERSONAL MIND MOVIE

Ex. The University of Notre Dame was playing at home versus Alaska Fairbanks during my freshman year. The rink always had a distinctive popcorn smell on game night that you could clearly smell on the ice. I was normally on the third line, but tonight I got moved onto the first due to an injury. The mind movie starts with a faceoff in the offensive zone on the blocker side of the goalie. The arena was jam packed and the band/student section were going crazy as I bent down to take the faceoff with a white knuckle grip on my stick. I closely watched the ref's hand drop the puck. As soon as his hand released the puck, I drove my stick into the opposing center's stick with as much force as I could muster, then I quickly swept the puck back to the Left D at the point. I keep my legs moving to fight off the opposing center and then busted to the net for a rebound. The puck deflects into the corner and my linemate rushes in to retrieve it. I take a quick look around to see the position of my teammates and position of the other teams' players in the zone. I break behind the net with two long strides and holler at my winger to cycle it back behind the net. He banks the puck off the boards and I notice the other teams defenseman break down to cover my position. I reach the puck first, set myself for the D's hit and feel my shoulder bang the glass so hard that it sways backward. I get low and spin off the hit by driving my feet while protecting the puck. I feel my skates cut into the ice as I beat the defenseman around the net. All the time I have my head up watching my wingers and D move for offensive position. I hear my left winger Ben Simon holler and I hit him with a perfect pass for a one timer. I fight toward the net, hit the D and battle for the rebound that is lying on the doorstep. I give everything I have to get to that rebound. I win the battle and lift the puck into the net and watch the twine bulge. I scored the go-ahead goal with 2 minutes left in the game. I am so pumped that all I can do is raise my hands and wait for the rest of the guys to come in and congratulate me. All five guys join the group huddle, happy as heck, saying anything that comes to mind. At this point I hear the siren blasting over the loudspeakers, the fans banging on the glass, and the band striking up the fight song. Unbelievably awesome. I skate hard toward our bench and high-five the entire team.

This is just one of the 10 mind movies that I would go through before each game. There should be another 9 mind movies highlighting different areas of your game to also go through. Just as before when you initially created and wrote them down, you will also go through an extended version while in a relaxed state- first in slow motion, then game speed, and lastly in fast forward. Here's what you may feel and experience---using my example above---at the different speeds.

Slow Motion

The above example was everything I felt in slow motion and it takes about 1 minute to do the mental walk through.You will actually feel the hits, faceoff win, spinning off the D, and the battle in front. You will want to move faster through the mind movie (game speed), but resist this urge and absolutely feel/experience each step of the play. This permanently implants the image and feelings into your brain, so later when you want a quick reference you will feel the same sensations as before. Once you have completed the mind movie in slow motion once then move on to Game Speed.

Game Speed

Start the play from the beginning and go through its entirety again in game speed. This should come naturally now. Of course you won't be able to feel, hear, smell, and see all the things that you would in slow motion but it will be there in your subconscious mind. Move through the play with confidence knowing that the play ends with a huge accomplishment. Focus on the big aspects of the play such as winning the draw, spinning away from the defenseman, hitting the open man, getting to the rebound first, and watching it go into the net. This will take 10-15 seconds max. Do this once and move on to play it in fast forward.

Fast Forward

At this speed the play should move at least twice as fast as normal. This will take under 5 seconds each time to run the entire play. Do this 3 times. You will only be able to see the play, where as the prior two scenarios you really felt the play with your entire body. Focus on two main parts of the play. This would be hitting the open man and watching the puck go into the net. You did this perfectly in the slow motion and game speed version. Permenantly stamp this image into your brain.

Step 3: Let it go

After completing the 10 "mind movie" visualizations in slow motion, game speed, and fast forward, then simply forget about them. We will focus on other methods such as routines and breathing that blocks outside distractions and also manufactures positive emotions to enhance your game. This step is completed after the final mind movie. The confidence established through this exercise will stay with you throughout the entire game. (You will quickly go through each mind movie in fast forward if you choose, in between the pregame skate and the game, to refresh them in your mind as you will see below.) If you continue to think about the upcoming game and worry about the other team for the entire time leading up to the game then you lack the moment-to-moment focus needed to get psyched up for the game. **Pressure to perform is created by anxieties about the future and remembered failures from the past.** In the present moment there is no pressure- only the now. Also if you overanalyze a certain situation, then some people (most people I know) get stuck on it and begin to even think the task is too big. This is called paralyzation by analyzation. Let it go and trust your subconscious mind to do the heavy lifting for you. You need to trust in your skills. Don't mentally make a mountain out of a mole hill.

Refreshing the Highlights from Your Mind Movie Right Before Game time

After highlighting the fact that you need to let it go after the initial visualization process, I'm going to give you the option(works for most people) of bringing it back briefly- right before the game if you're fortunate enough to have a pre-game skate. After the pre-game skate clock ticks down, after you have ripped the 100th puck at the crossbar, put the pucks in the paint bucket, and the zamboni doors open, you get back into the locker room, grab a cup of gatorade, sit down in your stall, and throw out a few "let's go boys." Then you have about 5 minutes before the coach comes into the locker room. You can quickly zip through all 10 mind movies in fast forward. Focus, just as you did before on the two most important moments in the play. Feel the confidence these moments create and smile. YOU'RE FORTUNATE ENOUGH TO BE PLAYING HOCKEY(always remember that), and now you're more mentally prepared then ever to help the team when the opportunity presents itself.

HOW TO GET OVER A SLUMP

"A slump starts in your head and winds up in your stomach. You know that eventually it will happen, and you begin to worry about it. Then you know you're in one and it makes you sick." – Billy Williams, a batting coach with the Chicago Cubs

I know that you have experienced the incredibly frustration of being in a slump. It sucks. Losing sleep over another game without a goal or point can drive you mad. "It's just a game," everyone says. But you just broke you're 200 dollar stick out of frustration by smashing it against the boards. Now you have another problem because either your dad or the trainer is going to ninja chop you in the neck for the broken twig. It's all bad...........

I'm just going to assume that everyone reading this book has been in a slump at onetime in their life. Whether in hockey, baseball, or dating it all starts with a couple of "unlucky breaks" and pretty soon it turns into a pattern that is hard to break. It's a natural cycle in sports that every player goes through. First you change your equipment, then you start gripping your stick harder, and finally you feel like nothing can go right. It's a tough position to be in when you can't see the light at the end of the tunnel. You get negative and think it will never end. You overanalyze everything and get into your head too much. Every time you see an opportunity to score or make the right play, your mind immediately thinks that you can't do it. I know, I've personally been there more than a few times. It's called a negative loop to the psychologically-minded doctors. You see an opportunity, you have a negative thought about it not turning out in your favor, you live up or rather down to the negative thought, and you're in the same exact spot you started. Now you just have another instance to think back to for proof that you suck. The following sidebar is a quick analysis of what you go through in a slump.

The Anatomy of a Slump

"A Slump is like a fire. It starts with a simple spark and can spread out of control if not contained." Cleveland Indians baseball psychologist

Digging Yourself a Hole(this usually happens over a 1-3 game stretch): A slump starts with consecutive bad games or missing a couple of routine plays. As an example of the escalating steps leading to a slump let's all put ourselves in the skates of a rock solid goaltender.***(Realizing goaltenders go into bad slumps always helped me as a forward. This means that you can shoot from anywhere and have the chance to score. You never know when the opposite netminder is in a bad funk and any sort of mental edge you give yourself will help.)*** As the number #1 goaltender for a team, you're going to be looked upon to start 80-90% of a team's games, perhaps more. To be up for each game requires tremendous mental strength. If for 1 period or even 5 minutes your mental concentration lapses and they score 2 or 3 quick goals, you get pulled. Now you have to sit on the bench with the towel around your neck, hat pulled low, and relive each goal. Your coach and entire team doesn't say a word, let alone even look at you. You know and they know you're better than that. The team can't climb back from the 3 goal deficit and gives up two points in the standings. Not to mention your personal save percentage craters. That night you go home with the loss resting on your shoulders, vowing to try harder and make it up next game.

Mind Bending Irritation(2-4 games): The team doesn't play for two days, so you vow to fix the mistakes in practice. "That was a fluke. No big deal" you tell yourself. The coach gives you the start because both he and the team have faith in your ability. The game starts with your team outshooting the other team big time and the puck is kept down in their end all except for a few outside shots. Then they have one big rush and the next thing you know you're fishing the puck out of the back of the net. The first thought that goes through your head is "Oh no not again. Now I'm going to have to play on my head just to keep my team in the game." (Trying harder leads to overthinking, overcommitting, and overplaying in this instance.) Before you know it you let in a few more and dig your team a deeper hole. Now your head starts playing tricks on you. Your muscles tighten and you begin to play tentatively/ Everyone in the building can see it. The fans cheer when you stop a slow roller from the redline and you don't laugh or break a smile in response. It's trouble.

Hair Pulling/Stick Breaking....Slump(after 4-5 games and lasts until you can break out of it): You don't understand what happened to your game. It's not a physical breakdown of your technique, but you still spent 30 minutes after the next 3 practices working on fundamentals. On top of questioning yourself, the coach sits you down and asks if there's a problem you need to talk about. You feel like slashing him in the face but simply say "no." You pull back from your teammates and forget about laughing at all the practical jokes in which you were a constant player only 10 days ago. You have thoughts common in these situations such as "if only I would have done this," "Why is this happening to me right now?" and "Do I deserve to be the Number 1 goaltender?"

Everyone says that you will break out of it. You just need to play through it or try harder. This worked in the past but somehow now it's a bigger obstacle then any you've ever faced. You've been in a slump before just like every other player in the locker room so you know it will eventually end. But when............. I'm going to show you how to stop it sooner by recognizing the steps and taking preventive measures to break free.

What you saw happening to the fictional goaltender is some of the same escalating steps you've gone through. The trick is if you can consciously recognize the steps then you can take preventative counter-steps to mitigate the slump and break out of it.

*****Just by sheer odds the number of goaltenders reading this will be far outnumbered by forwards or defenseman. I really don't want anyone(even goaltenders) to relive a slump. Just thinking about it will frustrate the H%ll out of you. But I know that we've all been there and can recognize the common pattern. *****

How To Get Over a Slump or a Dehabiliting Image

"This young man has had a very trying rookie season, with the litigation, the notoriety, his subsequent deportation to Canada and that country's refusal to accept him, I guess that's more than most 21-year-olds can handle. Number six. Ogie Ogelthorpe."
Slapshot -----(1977)

I don't like to spend a lot of time dredging up negative experiences because I believe the more you focus on something the more you bring this into your life. It's like the speeding car wrapped around the only telephone pole within a quarter mile. How did this happen? Because the driver lost control of his car and during the choas he focused on the only thing he needed to miss. The pole. But I also know that everyone has that last second mistake that cost their team the game, or the bad injury that you can't get out of your head, or the mental block that causes constant anxiety and poor performance in a certain situation. It's usually not as bad as in baseball or golf where you have the time to think over every play, but it can still be just as dehabiliting. Every time your mind thinks of a particular situation, which seems like every second in a slump, you have a rush of negative emotions. This is severely affecting your game. You know it and everyone around you can sense it. So let's get rid of them.

Now that you know some of the common escalation steps, as seen before in the goaltender situation, and the overall mindset behind nearly every slump, then you can use specific techniques to fight it. There are two ways to break the negative mind loop and erase the mental image of the nuclear meltdown, worst case scenario, that you imagine. In both options the goal is to gradually eliminate the bad thought from your mind. It's stuck there because of the importance you place on it and the strong negative emotions you feel everytime it runs through your mind. It's no way to prepare for a game. And it's definitely not a thought you want popping into your head at anytime during the action of the game. Once you complete one or both of the slump busting options below, you will literally laugh at the sticking point. It will simply fade away or be replaced by one of your positive "mind movies" implemented earlier.

Option A

"I made the joyous discovery that ten minutes of genuine belly laughter had an anesthetic effect and would give me at least two hours of pain-free sleep,"—Norman Cousins, a writer diagnosed with ankylosing spondylitis, he used only laughter and Vitamin C to live another 26 years.

This process is meant to be fun and produce a laugh or at least a smile instead of the "I suck so bad that my dog hates me" original feeling. It involves changing the bad image popping into your mind through a number of different comical ways.

Step 1: First, recall the bad image and put it into a "mind movie" format. If you're stuck in a slump then you've seen the image play out at least 100 times. Most likely it's the same dreaded thought each time. One more time isn't going to hurt. This exercise will eventually eliminate it, but first bear with me and rerun the negative images one more time.

Step 2: Since you've played this image out in your mind at least 100 times, it's grown into a monster of what was once a simple mistake. Realize that you're the director of your thoughts. You added things, including emotions and self talk, to this play until it's become a negative spiral severely effecting your game. Your mind made an action movie on the ice into a horror movie that would cause a small child to cry for a week afterwards. The good part about this is that you can put anything you want into this mind movie. Your new goal is to create a comedy of the situation. Rerun the situation, but this time make it a **CARTOON** instead of real life. Think South Park. (It's alright to laugh. That's the point of the exercise.)

Step 3: Now the slump causing movie is a cartoon playing in your head. Make one player Cartman from South Park, one player Peter from Family Guy, and the other player Homer Simpson. If there are more players, create them based on your favorite comedy shows. (This may seem ridiculous but obviously nothing else seems to work so give it a try. You might just end up laughing.)

Step 4: Now that you have the cartoon movie playing with you're favorite bunch of wacky characters, you can add a new scene. It doesn't have to have anything to do with your original negative loop. Grab your hockey stick and take a massive hack at Cartman's shins like Harry and Llyod in Dumb and Dumber. Or maybe rip a slapper off of Cartman's family jewels. This should bring a laugh to your face when you imagine it.

Step 5: The next step is to put the entire sequence together and play it forward in game speed. Remember you're the director of this thought. Do this at least 10 times. Make sure you have a smile on your face before stopping. Instead of the negativity previously felt while thinking about your slump, you can now shrug it off with a good laugh. It's very hard to be afraid of something that you can laugh at. It's like a "Kick Me" sign on the back of someone much bigger than you. It's very hard to fight the urge and not wind up and giv'r.

Step 6: This step will put the finishing touch on your new comedy. Take the complete mind movie that you played with all the new additions included in the prior 5 steps and now play it backwards 10 times in slow motion.

After you complete these 6 steps—or more if you feel like getting creative---you will erase the brain pathway of the old image and create this new one. Many people can do it just once and have it be enough. But for others, including myself, it takes repeating the process a couple times (or even more) to fully engrain the new thought into your head and replace the old one. Similar to the positive "mind movies", the key is to really see it clearly. Believe it or not if you can laugh about the new image then the slump is nearly broken. It's that simple because a slump is purely mental. This will allow you to play in the present the next game instead of holding onto mistakes from the past. When you play in the present you can fall back on your talent and work ethic to lift you out of the slump. Remember the great players make mistakes too- they just don't hold onto them as long. The trick is to detach yourself from the play, learn from it and then forget it. This first option involved laughter and the next option will be a serious way to eliminate these images.

Option B

"I am an old man and have known a great many troubles, but most of them never happened" --Mark Twain

I read about this option from NLP(Neurolinguistic Processing) therapists. It may seem a bit quirky but it works. I used this to get over my fear of sharks- not even remotely related to hockey but more terrifying to me than having my gloves accidently fall off while skating by George Larouqe. I watched Jaws when I was a kid and was afraid to even go water skiing in the lakes of Minnesota- absolutely froze me with fear. Just as the hockey obstacle is stuck in your head causing you massive problems, this fear was amplified to an irrational point. Do I know for a 100% fact that Lake Minnetonka doesn't have Great White's swimming around in it? **YES**. Was I hesitant to jump into the water in the middle of the lake? **YES**. In turn, do you think that you will never score a goal again? **OF COURSE NOT**. The point is that your emotions are very strong. Our minds tend to link thoughts together and create something out of nothing. This distorts reality and makes the current situation you're feeling the most important, all consuming thing in the world. But is it reality? You can use your rational self to downplay the scenario. It's called Reframing a belief. I believe this technique goes right to the core and pushes the thought from your mind. It may take more thought and time than Option A, but the results are just as powerful. After doing this technique a few hundred times, I was able to scuba dive and surf in parts of Australia and California where Great Whites were seen in the exact same spot within a week's period. This time, I knew that there were probably multiple Great Whites bigger than my car within a 2-mile radius. Was I a little scared floating on a piece of styrofoam camoflouged in a wetsuit so my pudgy body looked like a seal? Yeah for sure, but I still got over it and ended up having a great time. It's the same thing with your mental block concerning hockey.This option uses your prior experiences and knowledge to dismiss the worst case scenario running through your head. Let's get over it so you can go back to having fun and scoring goals.

Step 1: Get into a relaxed state, just as before with the visualization sequence. Use either the muscle flexing technique, regular breathing pattern, or simply listen to your favorite music to get calm and focused.

Step 2: Now re-run the negative scenario causing the slump. It's going to be tough, but you have to actually examine the root cause of what's getting you down. Pinpoint the exact thought and fear creating the internal state affecting your game. For example you've missed 5 open nets and haven't scored in 10 games, or you've been minus 9 in the last 5 games as a Defenseman, or you can't stop a beachball as a goalie. Bring the "I'll never score again" thought to the surface. When broken down this is the limiting belief that's holding you back.

Step 3: **NOW REFRAME THAT BELIEF.** It's a NLP(Neuro Linguistic Processing) technique used by psychologists to challenge beliefs, break unuseful associations, and create new possibilities. I'm going to walk you through 7 different ways of reframing the limiting belief using a forward's scoring drought as the example.

1. Reframe the External Behavior (not scoring): True you haven't scored in 10 games. Have you had opportunities to score? You will go through scoring droughts just as a baseball player will go through hitting droughts. If the baseball player hits the cover out of the ball and it finds the infielders glove, is it a slump? If you have 2 seeing eye goals in a game but play awfully are you happy? The key is to get consistent opportunities and the scoring will come.Take your mind off of scoring and focus on getting opportunities. It will come.

2. Reframe the Internal State(Negative feeling toward not scoring): You're in a slump and think you will never score again. Every thought about hockey or even going to the rink is negative. I don't have to tell you this isn't the starting point to break out of the slump. Begin to look for positives in your game besides scoring. A great back check to save a goal or a great hit for instance. Celebrate the little things and stick to the basics.This will encourage you and develop confidence.

3. Counter Example: Can you think of a time when you were in a similar situation? Can you think of a time when a teammate or even Alexander Ovechkin or Wayne Gretzky was in a similar situation? Everyone including yourself has been held scoreless for a number of games. Did you eventually score? Obviously.

4. Outcome Framing: What's going to happen on the ice if you keep thinking this way? You know how it's affecting your play now. Just think 5, 10, 20 games from now. It becomes a bigger obstacle every time you step on the ice. Will thinking this way help you score in that big game half a season away?

5. Allness Framing: I used this particular one to get over my fear of sharks in Australia. "More people are killed by bees then sharks." It's a fact. There are millions of people swimming in the ocean safely everyday. I shouldn't be paralyzed with fear if millions of other people are doing the exact same thing.

Along the same line of thinking- there are thousands of players scoring goals every night. Do you think that every player that has ever experienced a scoring slump went the rest of his career without scoring a goal? That's ridiculous.

6. Apply This Thought to Another Player on your Team or even Your favorite NHL Player: Do you think that because your linemate hasn't scored in ten games that he will never score again? If so why would you pass him the puck or want to ever play with him again? If the announcer notified you that your favorite NHL player hasn't scored in 10 games, what's the thought that goes through your head. He's due, right? *(This will get you into trouble in blackjack but feel free to think it about hockey.)*

This really highlights the ridiculous lengths that your mind goes to in a slump.

7. Chunk Down: This applies to the above section on The

Analogy of a Slump with the fictional goalie. How does a player get into a slump? How does it go from a few bad breaks and get magnified into a slump in your mind? What are the steps? How can you interrupt the pattern? If you can identify the steps than you can fight them.

At first, read through all 7 reframing techniques. You can use all 7 together or just focus on a particular one. Whatever works for you. The goal is to logically attack the notion that the slump will never end. Your mind has blown something small out of proportion and this exercise proves that to you. You will score again. You will get a shutout again. You will come from behind to win again. You will break out of the slump. It's not a question of if, but when.

"Whether **you think** that **you can**, or think that **you can**'t, **you** are usually right"
-- Henry Ford.

Both options above will work for any slump. The next time you step on the ice and encounter a situation or opportunity similar to the slump your subconscious mind will instantaneously play that positive "mind movie" of you scoring the goal, blocking the shot, winning the draw, etc. This will be the first thought your mind draws upon instead of the negative one holding you back. Then the negative loop is broken. ***In hockey it only takes a fraction of a second to make the right or wrong decision. And when you score or make the right play this will build real world confidence.***

Summary of the Visualization Chapter

- Visualization is the ability to see your self positively completing or reliving a scene only in the mind.

- It's been proven to mentally raise a players confidence, decrease anxiety/fear, and physically improve his performance in the specific visualized area.

- The most common form of visualization is seeing yourself completing a specific task in the future. We're going to use it for hockey by visualizing scoring goals, making the big save, winning the last second face-off, etc.

- You already use visualization everyday whether you know it or not. When you lie in bed on Sunday night and think about everything you have to do that week. When you think about what you're going to say to the cute girl sitting beside you in English class. When you go to the grocery store and plan the night's/week's meals. When you think about the weekend's hockey games. These are all some form of visualization. You will get deeper and clearer thoughts by practicing visualization techniques regularly.

- Limits begin where vision ends. The problem with most people is they think negative thoughts about future activities. The only surefire way for success is to stay positive.

- "80/20 rule"--Nearly everything in life falls under this concrete rule. Applied to hockey this means that 20% of the on-ice actions you take make up 80% of the results. Use this rule to narrow down what you want to visualize about.

- The most important aspect of visualizing is that you hav to actually feel the experience in all of your relevant senses- sight, hearing, touch, and smell. The more intense and real the feeling, the greater the impression is created on the brain

Visualization involves 3 Steps

1. **Relaxing the body and mind**
   a)Muscle relaxation
   b)Breathing Exercises
   c)Listen to Relaxing Music

2. **Visualization**
   a)Vividly experience the "10 mind movies"
      I. Slow Motion
      II. Game Speed
      III. Fast Forward

3. **Let it Go**

Slumps are mental obstacles that have become bigger than life for the person going through it. It's a negative loop.

There are two ways to get out of a slump:

1. Cure it through laughter.
2. Reframe the belief 7 different ways.

Breathing

Breathing

"In the four years I spent at Harvard Medical School and a year of internship in San Francisco, I learned nothing of the healing power of breath. I learned about the anatomy of the respiratory system, and I learned about diseases of the respiratory tract. But I learned nothing about breath as the connection between the conscious and unconscious mind, or as the doorway to control of the autonomic nervous system, or about using breathwork as a technique to control anxiety and regulate mental states, or the possibility that breath represents the movement of spirit in the body and that breathwork can be a primary means of raising spiritual awareness."[10]
---- Andrew Weil, director of the Program in Integrative Medicine and clinical professor of internal medicine at the University of Arizona in Tucson

Tyler Durden: [*pointing at an emergency instruction manual on a plane*] You know why they put oxygen masks on planes?
Narrator: So you can breathe.
Tyler Durden: Oxygen gets you high. In a catastrophic emergency, you're taking giant panicked breaths. Suddenly you become euphoric, docile. You accept your fate. It's all right here. Emergency water landing - 600 miles an hour. Blank faces, calm as Hindu cows.
Fight Club—(1999)

"Regulate the breathing, and thereby control the mind." ---- Yoga master B.K.S. Inyengar

A great way to control a negative emotional response and minimize its effect comes from learning how to breathe correctly. Taking deep breaths and thus getting more oxygen into the body will slow your heart rate, decrease perspiration and relax the muscles. Breathing Patterns can be used to counteract the internal changes your body goes through in stressful situations. Our

[10] http://www.healingmoves.com/carol/articles/breathe.html

bodies do this naturally when you sigh in relief. This chapter focuses specifically on how breathing affects the body and certain techniques practiced for thousands of years to improve the body's response to stressful situations.

I'm sure you've all heard these statements from one coach or another along the way.

"Just relax out there guys and have some fun"
"Quick shifts and get off"
"Maintain your composure"
"Backcheck hard"
"This faceoff is the game"
"You're gripping your stick too hard"

All of these statements in one way or another directly relate to your breathing. It's a pretty simple concept and I trust that everyone reading this book can do it. But in reality many of us -including myself- take quick shallow breaths. This gives us just enough oxygen to supply our body in a relaxed state. Shallow breathing may cut it when you're lying on the couch laughing at Wedding Crashers for the 50th time. However it's not going to cut it when you're chasing a 6 oz. rubber puck on a 185' by 85' foot surface of frozen water. Most people only use about twenty percent of their lung capacity and seventy percent of waste elimination from your body is through breathing. So why is it that something that is so simple to do, that requires no other tool other than our own bodies is so neglected. My theory is that we have been programmed to believe that nothing as simple and easy as breathing could possibly make that much of a difference.[11] As a result people take quick breaths like they have all their life and fail to use the bottom portion of their lungs. And any time we feel stress (basically every shift of every game) our muscles become tense, our heart beats accelerate and our breathing becomes erratic. This further

---

[11] http://breathing.com/articles/oxygen-benefits.htm

reduces the oxygen getting into your blood stream and tires you out.

Deep breaths, short breaths, holding your breath, breathing through your nose, exhaling through your mouth, focused breath, belly breaths, chest breaths... This was all new to me when I first started to learn the different ways to breathe. I just thought your brain had this one under control. The only time I even considered breathing differently is when I was on the wrong end of a buddy pass and got the wind knocked out of me. That next breath felt a million miles away. But do you know that manipulating your breath can have a huge impact on your body? The truth is- breathing can have a profound effect on your hockey game- including positive, internal chemical changes. Many athletes currently use specific breathing techniques to get a leg up on their competition. It can be used to increase energy, reduce stress, and mentally focus, as well as a huge range of other benefits. These benefits have been studied for thousands of years and are used extensively in Eastern martial arts. Breathing is said to promote a calm, lucid, free state of mind that leads to victory. We will focus on breathing before the game to get you into "The Zone" mentally and other techniques to provide energy and focus needed for a great game.

Many forms of breathing techniques exist. They all provide a way to positively change your internal state, which leads to a relaxed mental state. The goal is to use the following breathing exercises at specific times before the game and then during the game to improve performance. This will help get you into the zone and stay in the zone.

Any sport produces stress throughout the contest and hockey produces more than most. Every defensive zone face-off is a chance for your man to score. Every time you have the puck, you can either create a great offensive play or pull a bonehead move resulting in a turnover. Not to mention that every member on the other team is trying to physically maim you. And then throw on top of that expectations from friends and family. **Each player responds differently to stressful situations.** Some people are cardiac responders, where their heart rate goes up. Some people retreat mentally and listen to the fearful voice inside their head that questions their ability. Some people are skin responders-their palms sweat, sweat gets into their eyes, and their skates weigh a sweat logged 10 pounds after the game. Other players' muscles tighten and they forget to breathe. Think for a second about the position that produces the most stress- the goalie. Of all the goalies you played with, how many had a screw loose upstairs? Whether you consciously think about these stressful situations or not, it creates a great deal of strain on the body and mind. Not only before the game, but also during and after. This section isn't about eliminating the stress, which is impossible, but rather controlling its effect on your body by breathing differently. Gary Mack from the book Mind Gym writes this "Oxygen is energy---it's juice. Oxygen helps relax muscles and clear the mind. When you hold your breath, you are creating pressure and a nervous feeling. Athletes who choke start to become nervous about being nervous. Anxious about being anxious." One psychologist says anxiety is excitement "without the breath." Being in a relaxed state allows you to enter the game without feeling any mental/physical obstacles so you just play. Relaxation provides a mind-body integration that leads to optimal performance." [12]

Shoot-out Preparation

"Anika has been able to control the heart beat and control the emotions. There is only one way to calm the heartbeat and that is with the breathing." Peter Kostis, commentator for CBS sports talking about Anika Sorenstam's first tournament on the men's PGA Tour

"If you think, you're dead" --- Top Gun (1986)

[12] *Mind Gym*, Gary Mack and David Casstevens, McGraw- Hill, 2001

Tiger Woods stands over a 15 foot snake of a putt to win the tournament. Everything slows down for him. He calmly goes through his routine, all the while controlling his breathing. He sinks the putt and wins the tournament. They say that the golf ball is only in contact with your club for under a second the entire round. *(More when mulligans are included, but who's counting*?) This leaves a lot of time to rethink your past shots and over think your next shot. Hockey is very different. It's such a fluid game that everyone on the bench makes a meaningful contribution to a win or a loss. There are very few individual plays such as a free throw in basketball, field goal kick in football, or a single pitch in the bottom of the ninth with bases loaded and a 3-2 count. There are also very few times when the game slows down enough to stop and think about the next play before it actually happens. It's very hard to get nervous on a breakaway or a 2-1 for long because it will be over in seconds. But since the new rule changes, games and whole seasons are being decided with the shootout format. Say what you want about leaving everything on the ice for 65 minutes only to have it be decided by a shootout, but the fans love it and it's definitely here to stay. This does however provide the rare individual play with enough time to actually produce those uneasy butterflies in your stomach- Kind of like standing over a golf putt with 30 million beer-chuggin Canadians watching. The quickest way to remove distractions and refocus your mind is through breathing.

This breathing exercise will provide physical and mental energy to your body and mind which is drained from the regulation/OT. It will also provide a calming focus needed because the games' outcome rests on your shoulders. I mean after all, the two points are up to you to win for your team. You need to score and you have less than 5 minutes to prepare.

The breathing exercise to use at this moment is called "Circle Breathing." Start by inhaling through your nose for 3 seconds. This needs to be a deep breath, so make sure to feel your stomach expanding when inhaling. Mentally follow the breath inhalation from your nose down to your rising stomach.

Hold the breath for 3 seconds. Picture it staying in the center of your body right behind the belly button. Then exhale through your mouth for 5 seconds by pulling your stomach in. Picture the air coming back up and out of your mouth. By following your breath this will take your mind off of the coming shot and bring you into the moment. You can trust your skills (The coach chose you over other players on the team), erase any doubts, and not fear the outcome. This is the zone you need to be in.
THE PRESENT…………………

*****I realize that the above and below techniques may seem a little weird and you might get chirped by your teammates if you use them. That's alright. Trust me it will make you better. Be confident enough to approach this with a positive attitude and willingness to practice anything that will make you better. If it makes you feel any better you can do these techniques on your own in a quiet corner and the breathing exercises that can be used during a game won't be noticed anyways. Everyone will be in their own thoughts about the game or listening to the coach. Don't be afraid to be a leader and do things on your own. *****

Flexible Breathing

The second breathing exercise for you is called Flexible Breathing. The idea of the Flexible Breathing technique is to stretch your lungs a little bit beyond your comfort level, allowing you to ultimately take in more oxygen. This will cut down on your struggle for breath in intense game situations. It's also useful to increase your energy level and improve your metabolism. Ideally, you should begin this process at least two weeks before practices start, so you will be in better breathing condition and therefore "suffer" less during bag skates and long games. It would be beneficial-once you have some practice using this breathing technique-to do 5-10 minutes of Flexible Breathing before the game, so your lungs will be stretched and ready for the up and down action.

Exercise 1. Flexible Breathing (Continued Practice Everyday/Pre-game)

How to Use Flexible Breathing:

Step 1: Begin by sitting in a comfortable position, with your back straight, and your chest puffed out. Put one hand on your stomach and the other hand on your side. Do about one minute of regular, natural deep breathing to warm up. In this normal breathing pattern, you're going to gradually expand the lungs. As you inhale, imagine your lungs filling up with air from the bottom of the stomach to the top - each exhale should be the exact opposite as you feel the breath leaving.
Step 2: After warming up with your regular breathing pattern, increase the amount of oxygen you inhale so you can feel the stomach expanding with your hand. Take as many breaths as necessary until it feels comfortable and smooth. Keep the breathing steady and balanced by always inhaling with the air filling your lungs from bottom-to-top and exhaling by pushing the oxygen out from top-to-bottom.
Step 3: Breathe again so the bottom of your stomach is expanded with air. Feel your entire chest filling up until it feels like your lungs are pushing against the bottom of your shoulders. Each breath inhalation should fill up your entire inner space, and each exhale should leave you feeling totally "collapsed" inside - literally "flat as a pancake".
Step 4: When you have this breathing pattern down, add a final step. As you inhale to the point where you can't take in any more air, breathe in just a little more air through your nose, so that you literally are full. This little extra intake of air will expand the

lungs with practice so in a game situation you will tire less easily. As you exhale, push out every single ounce of air, so that your chest feels completely collapsed.

As you will see below Big Wave surfers use this to expand their lungs because they're put into intense situations where they may not be able to breathe for up to a minute.

Initially, this technique will be tough, but like anything new, including the visualization, it will get easier with time and gradually become routine. If you feel lightheaded or dizzy at any time discontinue the exercise immediately and start breathing normally.

The Everest of Waves

In 1961, three surfers tied their pet dog to their car bumper and paddled out to an unknown break over a ½ mile from the beach. They struggled in the cold 10-foot waves and, after a couple of minutes, realized their dog, Maverick, was swimming right beside them. The dog always swam in the waves with them during their surf sessions, but this time the waves were too big for the surfers paddling on their huge boards, let alone a dog. So they decided to spend the rest of the day on the beach watching the monstrous waves crash into the huge rocks a ½ mile out. This became the first recorded attempt to surf the most dangerous wave in the world and the reason for their name, "Mavericks".

Of the tens of millions of surfers throughout the globe, only about 50 have had the courage, or some say stupidity, to venture out during the winter's big wave season. In order to even get into position in the lineup *(the bench in hockey terms),* the surfer must paddle for at least 45 minutes in bitterly cold water through intense currents, around jagged rocks in thick fog. And to top it all off, it's a great white shark playground where more than one surfer has been attacked. When you get to the lineup, which is a safe haven-except for the sharks- just outside the breaking waves, you wait with a group of other crazy people for a chance to ride a huge mountain of water (50 feet plus). If you decide to risk your life and go for it, you have to paddle as fast as humanly possible to put yourself in the right position to ride it. As soon as the wave jacks up and starts to lift you a minimum of 50 feet over the horizon, you must make the decision. Go or pull back. If you decide to risk you life and go, the wave presents you with a difficult challenge. It breaks in multiple areas. It's basically the scariest wave imaginable. As one surfer put it "I don't know why Mavericks doesn't kill people all the time."

Riding a wave at Mavericks is like dropping down the side of a 6-story building with an avalanche of water pushing you forward. The prospect of falling 35-feet straight down and having the equivalent of 10,000 Olympic pools being dumped on your head is awaiting you, should you make a mistake. The wipeouts are so devastating that surfers have described it as "a terrible car accident in a washing machine that is trying to rip off your arms." The power of the wave drives the surfers' 40-feet deep into pitch black water, ping-ponging him off rocks and the bottom. Its pitch black in this murky water, so there's no way to know which way is up. And the worst case scenario is being held under for a number of waves.

So imagine paddling as hard as you absolutely can for 15-20 seconds *(sprinting full speed down the ice)*, then jumping to your feet only to look down the edge of a 5-6 story drop (this alone would suck the breath out of me like a punch in the gut). If you make one tiny mistake, then you will drop from higher than an Olympic high dive. You most likely hit the water in an awkward position and get the wind knocked out of you. Then the curling wave sucks you back up and slams you down 40 feet below the surface. The force of the wave feels like it's ripping off your arms as you get dragged underwater over the equivalent of an entire football field for over a minute. To put it in a hockey perspective, imagine back checking up and down the ice then fighting Bob Probert and Tie Domi at the same time without being able to take a breath because this is all happening underwater. And that still doesn't do the wipeout at Mavericks justice.

Nearly every surfer at Mavericks has a tale of blacking out. Obviously breathing is a huge part of their training. Surfers practice for this particular scenario by doing all of the conventional training to get in great shape such as running, riding the bike, and swimming. They also do other things such as diving down 40 feet, picking up a 75 pound rock, and running along the bottom of the ocean for as long as possible. But also some of the surfer's main training involves breath expansion (Flexible Breathing) exercises leading up to the big wave season.

"First up be aware that the way we breathe can either lessen or make worse the emotional- fear response. Anxiety can be caused by a poor breathing technique. Anxiety can do seroius harm and even kill as any form of extreme emotion can. So reduce the anxiety, increase the oxygen, and live long time. Unless you have a serious unbalanced breathing problem then this exercise will help calm and energize you."

This next exercise is very similar to Flexible Breathing outlined above. It's referenced from a big wave surfer's travel journal on the site surftravelcompany.com:

Step 1: Sit down and be erect but not stiff, if you'd rather stand bend your knees slightly so as to unlock them. **Step 2:** Relax your jaw and let your gut go.

Step 3: Put your thumbs below your back just above your pelvis. This is the kidneys. Wrap your hands around your love handles with firm grip. Then while breathing through your nose, breathe in slow and lengthy for a three count. Allow it to expand your fingers, forcing them apart. Feel the tension. Take an extra gulp of air. **Step 4:** Now breathe out and count to seven. Be careful not to tighten your belly while you extend the breathing out. Just slow-down the speed of exhalation.

Do it again-- 3 count in-- 7 count out.

Warning: Now if you are getting dizzy or spaced out then rest a bit.[13]

Breathe Counting

The Third breathing technique is called Breath Counting. This exercise narrows your focus and gets rid of any negative thoughts before the game. You can use breath counting in conjunction with the visualization sequence. Ideally you should perform this breathing exercise in a quiet space before the game. But if that's impossible, grab your iPod, put on some relaxing tunes, and sit in the corner of the locker room. The object of the exercise isn't to become physically relaxed, but rather mentally relaxed so your complete focus is on the game ahead.

[13] http://www.surftravelcompany.com/BIG_WAVE_SURFING-BREATHING.htm

Exercise 2. Breath Counting (Pre-game/During Visualization Process)

How to Count Breaths:

Step 1. Start by finding a quiet space or else get lost in a mellow song on your iPod. Close your eyes and focus on one or all of the positive "mind movies" you created in the prior visualization chapter. This will put you in a positive state and provide a future goal to reach.

Step 2. Next push your tongue to the back of your front upper teeth. Exhale by making a hissing sound as the air goes around your tongue for 3 seconds. (It's very easy to do. Try it now.) The whistling sound brings your conscious mind to the present moment with every exhale. Don't ask. It's Yoga stuff that works.

Step 3. Now inhale through your nose for 4 seconds. Make sure that you feel your stomach rise as you do this. This will ensure that you're taking deep breaths, and your body is getting the maximum amount of oxygen possible.

Step 4. After inhaling, hold your breath in the bottom of your stomach for 6 seconds (just make sure it was longer than your inhalation). This will do two things:

1. Provide the maximum amount of oxygen to your muscles and brain for psychical benefits
2. Center your mind to focus completely on the game ahead.

(Combined with visualization techniques learned earlier, this will provide the focused intensity needed before a game.)

Step 5: Next, exhale through your mouth, with your tongue still pressed behind the top front teeth, for a total of 8 seconds. Repeat this exercise 5 times. You can do this exercise individually or use it in conjunction with the all of the breathing exercises.

During a quick downtime in a game, this technique, in a shortened version, can be used to focus on the present. Picture this- you're rearing to go and absolutely know you're going to dominate this team. Then you step on the ice in a tough visiting barn and all of a sudden the bright lights, crowd volume, and pure energy hit you like a Bob Probert right. Your brain can lose focus. Suddenly that calm energy you worked so hard to get all day before the game becomes an anxious/nervous energy. You can use the breath counting technique to quickly bring yourself back to the present and forget the bright lights and noise taking you off of your game. At this time, don't use the breathing technique as described above with the visualization "mind movies". Instead do a quick count of your deep stomach inhalations and full exhalations. This will help bring you into game ready focus and allow you to play up to your physical potential.

Quick Breaths

HOW TO GET A BOOST OF ENERGY USING BREATHING TECHNIQUES BEFORE A GAME

Now that you've focused on mentally and physically improving your body using breathing exercises before the game, let's focus on a breathing pattern that can be used to gain energy. I read about a similar exercise in an article about deep water diving. (A sport where they push the limits to the extreme. Kind of like seeing how many lengths you can swim in a pool, except you swim straight down to the black depths of the ocean, where the pressure is so great that your lungs compress to the size of your fist……..Not for me.) This is a great exercise developed through yoga that will increase your energy, called Quick Breaths. I've seen many players do a number of ridiculous things for extra energy before a game from eating an onion to drinking 3 red bulls. (Biting into an onion? Never got that one.) Of course, adding stimulants in the form of caffeine or any other drug will provide energy, but also have a negative side effect later on down the road. This offsets the positive effect, and in my opinion, causes physical strain on the body. (For instance, coffee is a diuretic- causing dehydration and possible cramping late in the game.) This breathing exercise, when done properly, will provide a boost of energy to start the game without your body crashing late in the game. It's a yoga technique and better option than reaching for a cup of coffee or a 24 oz. Rockstar.********Make sure to do this before the pre-game skate or at least 15 minutes before game time due to slight chance of getting dizzy.*************

Exercise 3: Quick Breaths(10 min. Pre-game)

Step 1: Sit in a comfortable up-right position with your back straight, and chest puffed out.

Step 2: With your mouth closed, breathe in and out of your nose as fast as comfortably possible. To give an idea of how this is done, think of using a bicycle pump to quickly pump up a tire. The upstroke on the bicycle pump is when you breathe in, and the down stroke is when you breathe out. Both are equal in length.

Step 3: The rate of breathing is quick, with as many as 2-3 sets of breathing in/out per second.

Step 4: While doing the exercise, you should feel a slight effort of the muscles at the base of the neck, chest and abdomen. These muscles will increase in strength as this technique is practiced more and more.

Step 5: In the beginning do this exercise no longer than 10 seconds at a time. With practice, slowly increase the length of the exercise by 5 seconds every week or so. Trust yourself. When you feel comfortable then up the exercise by 5 seconds. Do it as long as you are comfortable, but do not exceed 45 seconds.

******Just a note of caution:******* Using this exercise for an extended period of time when just beginning can cause hyperventilation. For this reason, it initially should be practiced while sitting down in a safe place. I'm being overly cautious but just be cool and smart about this or anything else people tell you to do. You know your limits better than anyone else.

(Warning: I feel like an adult mentioning this, but many kids--including some of my friends when I was younger-- played a game where you purposely tried to pass out. It's honestly the worst idea ever. You're cutting off oxygen to your brain, which could cause death or severe retardation. Never ever do this. You're smarter than that.)

The prior breathing exercises focused your mind, calmed your anxious nerves, and generated a quick boost of energy before a game. But how about the time when you get caught deep in your own zone for what seems like an hour, as the other team tic-tac-toes your line to death? They didn't score, but now you've been on the ice so long that your lungs are on fire and you're coasting to the bench hunched over with your stick resting on your knees. The 4th and final breathing exercise is called Low Breathing and it deals with the above problem. Low Breathing is meant to get your oxygen levels back to normal after a long shift.

Low Breathing

Hockey is a unique game. Players give their absolute max for 45-75 seconds then rest for a longer period. As a trained athlete you can operate at 75% to 85% max VO2 for short intervals. If you continue pushing your body past it's anaerobic threshold then acid will accumulate in the muscle cells of the body. This is when you muscles start burning. The quickest way to balance the acidity is to provide much needed oxygen to the cells. But breathing "normally" to catch your breathe, after a long shift, reduces the potential oxygen in your blood by up to 20%. Many times you further reduce oxygen intake, constricting your lungs by being hunched over on the bench breathing through your mouth. You may know it by the name sucking wind. After a tough drill in practice, watch how many guys lean against their sticks on the top of their shin pads. I was guilty of this little crutch after every skating drill. I just couldn't seem to catch my breath between drills. (Granted, as a fat kid, growing up I hated anything to do with running, but still I was in decent shape.) A big reason why I couldn't catch my breath was because the hunched over resting position I used was constricting my lungs' ability to take in oxygen. Also by breathing through my mouth, I couldn't regulate the air filling my lungs. Breathing through your nose filters out the impurities and regulates the temperature of the air. Makes a big difference in hockey where the average playing surface is way below freezing. So how can you breathe in a way to bring your body back to balance after gutting out a tough shift and also provide energy for the next shift? By using a technique called Low Breathing. When you come back to the bench after a long shift and you're trying to catch your breath, your coach is barking orders, and your teammates are giving you props for the sick toe drag, think "Low Breathing".

Exercise 4: Low Breathing (During the Game/Breath Recovery)

Step 1: Low Breathing starts with relaxed diaphragmatic breathing. Relax your stomach so that it can move outward and can expand full of air with each inhalation. Breathe in through your nose and expand your stomach as full as possible with air. To focus your mind, imagine the oxygen you're breathing in carries confidence or any other positive emotions you want to feel. This little trick can give you the mental edge for the next shift. It's also very important to feel the lower part of your stomach filling with air. This ensures you're inhaling the greatest amount of oxygen possible and the reason it's called Low Breathing.

Step 2: Don't hold that breathe in. (It will actually be very hard at first to slow down and breathe deeply on the bench after a long shift. It takes practice.) As soon as your "stomach" is full then exhale fully. Imagine the exhalation is carrying out all of the weakness, doubt, and worry built up in your body. You should feel like your stomach is pulling in toward your spine.

Repeat the process until your breath slows and you're fully recovered.

Explanation

I know diaphragmatic breathing sounds like a horrible procedure at your doctor's office. Your diaphragm is a muscle located below the stomach and works to control your breathing. It's the muscle that used to cramp up in that dreaded 1-mile run test in middle school. When you look at a picture of the lungs (see below) you can see that they're shaped like a pear.

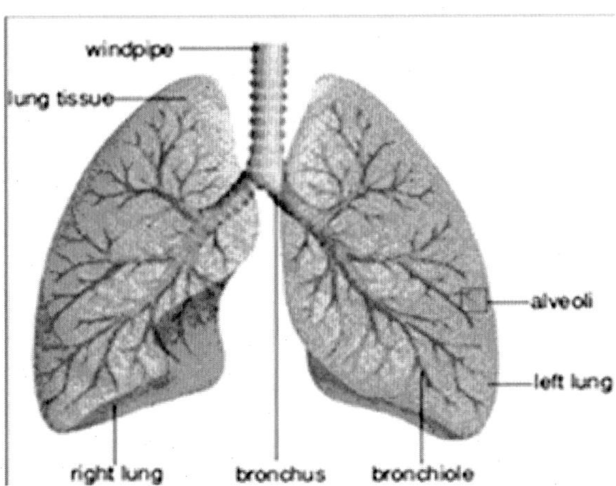

As you can see by the picture, the upper half contains a much smaller area of space for oxygen to enter the bloodstream. With short, quick breaths many people only use this area. As you can see the lower portion of the lungs contains twice as much area. You use this lower lung space by breathing deep and expanding the stomach with each breath. This allows more oxygen to reach the blood. The more oxygen that reaches the blood, the quicker you can recover and get yourself focused and back on the ice.

Summary of Breathing Chapter

- A great way to control a negative emotional response and minimize its effect comes from learning how to breathe correctly.
- Use deep breaths to expand and use the complete area of the lungs. Very few people-musicians, some athletes, and singers-do this.
- Use Circle Breathing to calm your nerves and bring yourself back to the present before a penalty shot.
- Breathing can have a profound effect on your hockey game including positive internal chemical changes.
- "Oxygen is energy---its juice. Oxygen helps relax muscles and clear the mind. When you hold your breath, you are creating pressure and a nervous feeling."

There are 4 Breathing Exercises to use for different results before and during a game.

1. Flexible Breathing—The idea behind this exercise is to stretch out the lungs so when you get caught deep in your own zone you have that extra breath of air to get you through. Remember the big wave surfers who consider this a crucial part of their training.

2. Breath Counting-- This exercise narrows your focus and gets rid of any negative thoughts before the game.

3. Quick Breaths— This exercise provides a boost of energy before the game.

4. Low Breathing-- Allows you to recover on the bench after a tough shift when you're sucking wind.

Controlling Your Emotions

Controlling Your Emotions

"When Jackie Robinson was verbally abused or when players slid into second base with their spikes high, Robinson kept his temper in check. He turned away, then got his revenge with a base hit, a diving catch, or a stolen base. It is easy to fight back, but it takes real courage to turn the other cheek and show your class and self-control." From an article explaining why Brooklyn Dodgers' general manager Branch Rickey chose Jackie Robinson as the right man to break baseball's color barrier by becoming the first African-American to play in the major leagues

"You do that, you go to the box you know, 2 minutes by yourself, you feel shame, then you get free." --- *Slapshot (1977)*

You haven't scored in 10 games and your teammate just set you up on the doorstep for an easy tap-in into an open net. Then the puck rolls off your stick wide or worse yet, you shoot it right back into the goalie's chest. On the way back to the bench you try to rearrange the boards with your 200 dollar stick. Hanging your head on the bench, all you can think of is the missed opportunity, which has already played itself in your head 5 times. "How could you miss that and Why can't you score, you idiot?" you ask yourself as well as a bunch of other statements that make South Park the movie sound tame. **This negative self talk will derail your game.**

For instance, have you ever had any of these feelings:

1. You were gripping the stick too hard
2. Passes were bouncing off your stick
3. You were missing the net at point blank
4. You were passing it into peoples' skates

...........and worst of all you couldn't control it?

It's the negative loop coming back to haunt you. Every negative emotion you feel feeds into the loop and keeps you in the same mental state. You believe you can't score, even on an open net, so you don't and this reinforces your thoughts. It drives you absolutely crazy. At this present moment you're what NHL scouts call a mental midget.

Your parents, coaches, teammates, friends, scouts, and most of all "yourself" expect near perfection every time you lace up the skates. Little stresses pile up until the game seems like climbing Mt. Everest and now every shift you're in a stressful state. It's literally impossible to perform in this condition. To get into this condition the body goes through a number of specific steps. Cortisol or what's commonly known as the "stress hormone" is being pumped out of your adrenal glands at high doses. During times of emotional stress, our sympathetic nervous system is stimulated and creates a number of changes within our body. Our heart rate rises, we perspire, our muscles tense, we have feeling of anxiety, increased stress, and our breathing becomes rapid and shallow. It gets so bad that in everyday life an estimated 90% of doctor visits are directly attributed to stress. You can only imagine what it's doing to your game out on the ice. Not good.

Stress can be used to your advantage in certain situations but if you let it spiral out of control the above side effects prevent you from playing up to your full potential. The trick is to consciously recognize and feel the emotions rising within you and then perform specific actions to temper them or else use them as an impetus to reach a higher energy level.

The emotions that I've felt during my career and I know you have too in no particular order include:

1. **Anger**
2. **Jealousy**
3. **Frustration**
4. **Fear**
5. **Defeated (Will to Win)**

As a player you've most likely felt all of these emotions at some time during your hockey career. The body was designed to feel these emotions because in the past they helped us-humans-survive. However in a hockey game these emotions just throw off your focus and your game ultimately suffers. Let's go through some examples of each emotion, including when you may have felt them, what it does to your game, and then what you can do to minimize the effect and turn them into a positive force.

Anger:

"What has benefited me the most is learning I can't control what happens outside of my pitching." -Greg Maddux, one of the greatest MLB pitchers of all time.

Anger is perhaps the most common emotion felt on the ice. Control is impossible in such a fast paced sport with over 40 different personalities colliding for 60 minutes on a small ice surface. Hockey is a fiercely competitive sport where both teams will do anything to win. This brings frustration from failing to meet expectations set by your coach and yourself. This is felt to a degree by every player in every game and creates anger. Anger is usually directed in two main directions- against the other team and worst of all at **YOURSELF**. In the first scenario, a player from the other team may take a cheap shot at you or a teammate. Your blood immediately boils over. If the ref didn't see it and there's no penalty, then it's even worse. All you can think about is getting revenge. **How many times have you heard the saying the retaliation act is the penalty which gets called?** Putting your team down a man for 2 to 5 minutes while you sit in the box hurts your team and your standing with the coach. If you let anger get the best of you, it usually brings out the worst in you. *(Wow, I must have pulled that one out of the back of my mind from some coach I had over a decade ago.)*

Ok. The first step after seeing/feeling something that gets you angry is to recognize that you're actually feeling it. It may take a few seconds or even as long as a minute to get out of the heat of the moment. Then you can evaluate if what you're feeling is beneficial going forward in the game. Great players in any sport have an inner gauge control. Tim Salmon, a MLB player said, "I can't control the pitcher, the ball, the fielders, or the crowd, so I must be in control of myself." Moving forward you have 2 options.

1. Calm yourself down, use patience and take the other players' number if you feel the need for payback, and get back to your game.

When you get angry, your emotions take over. It's like taking a drug. A number of chemicals flood your body in preparation for a fight. In order to neutralize these chemicals you must control your thoughts. This can be done through some of the breathing exercises mentioned in the prior chapter. For example by using deep breaths.

a. Start by inhaling for 4 seconds.
b. Hold the breath for 8 seconds. Feel all the anger in your body gather into a ball in your stomach.
c. Exhale for 16 seconds. As you exhale, feel the giant ball of anger in your stomach release and leave your body.
d. Continue to breathe in this pattern until you feel ready to play at the same emotional level you started the game.

2. Control the anger and use it as a motivation to push yourself to a higher level.

Have you heard of the expression "let sleeping dogs lie"? I remember my dad talking about Clarke Gillies, now in the Hall of Fame and one of the toughest fighters in the late 70's early 80's. Teams would shy away from him and let him be in the hope he wouldn't wake up to take over the game with his physical presence. He would channel his anger and use it against his opponents. Instead of anger ripping the game out of your hands, control it and use it as a motivation going forward.

a. First realize the anger you're feeling. It's raising specific chemicals within your body to trigger either a fight or flight response.
b. Obviously you're going to "fight" or stay in the game. The best option isn't to go after the other player and take a stupid penalty but rather use those chemicals running through your body, such as adrenaline, to your advantage.
c. With the mind movies in the Visualization section you know as a player what your strengths are. If your mind movies focus on scoring and offensive contributions to the team then going forward you direct your adrenaline to those situations. If your mind movies focus on solid D and big hits then get your team pumped up with a big open ice hit. You don't need to run around the ice trying to avenge something that made you angry. Stay within your game plan with these heightened emotions and you can hurt the other team where it really counts, on the scoreboard.

The other scenario mentioned above is the habit of getting down on **YOURSELF** because you're not playing up to the high standards you demand. Actually getting down on yourself may be worded too lightly. I don't know about you, but I personally wanted to break my stick over my own head more than a few times during a game. I was far from perfect and missed a few thousand passes, defensive assignments, and open nets. That will happen. You will fail; you will make big mistakes and small mistakes and everything in between. You're not perfect and guess what neither is Sidney Crosby. **After a mistake the only thing you can control is your reaction to it.** Every player has two competing voices in his head. One pushes you forward with positive uplifting comments and the other one creates doubt and fear. Unfortunately most players listen to the latter, negative voice. This affects how you feel and how you feel is how you're going to play. Only you can control your emotions. This anger at yourself must be put behind you immediately. **Say this over and over again with me. There is nothing I can do now to change the past. All I can do is use it as a lesson and play better in the future.** If you find yourself getting angry or down during a game try these four steps.

1. Stop and recognize the feeling.
2. Use the breathing technique from above, or use an anchor-which you will learn about later in the chapter, or use a fast forward or a mind movie to refocus your thoughts. The breathing and anchor techniques will slow down the surging adrenaline in your body. The mind movie will create confidence.
3. Learn the lesson from the mistake(DON'T pass up the middle, DO tie up your man's stick in front of the net, DO hit the net, etc.)
4. Let it go and realize you're bigger than 1 or 10 mistakes. As long as you have a next shift somewhere in the future then you can redeem yourself.

The trick is to forget about your mistakes and celebrate your successes no matter how small. This will keep the positive voice louder than the negative.

Fear:

F. alse **E.** vidence **A.** ppearing **R.** eal

"Fear is the worst hazard because it creates tension, doubts, and even panic."---Sam Snead, a professional golfer.

This is not an emotion we associate with hockey, but I'll be the first one to admit I've experienced it more times than I can remember. Almost every athlete faces this emotion over the course of their career. In fact, according to the book *The Toughest Men in Sports* by Mike Chapman, which details the champions of wrestling, martial arts, and boxing over the past 100 years, only Rocky Marciano never displayed or even talked about having any sort of fear. Every other fighter including Muhammad Ali had to overcome this obstacle.[14] Fear comes in many forms including fear of a bigger/better opposing team, fear of losing, not playing your best, getting injured, disappointing a family member/fan/coach, or fear of success. It can physically paralyze you at its worst and be described as butterflies in your stomach when felt to a lesser degree. It's usually disguised as nervousness when given a name, and I will be the first to agree that not labeling it as fear will help. But whatever label you give it, the key is to eliminate that feeling as quickly as possible or use it as a positive force to push you forward. Just as anger produces a chemical reaction in the body that affects performance, so does fear. When fear takes over you concentrate on the negative and play tentatively hoping that you can hide from your fears. Instead let's focus on eliminating the fears. Here's how:

Fear is one of the most basic responses for any normal animal or human walking the earth. It's a response to a perceived threat. Without fear, you would cross a busy street without looking, pinch Brock Lesnar's girlfriend's butt as she walks by,

---

[14] *Toughest Men in Sports: Looking for the Mental Edge,* Mike Chapman, Culture House, 2001

or play dodgeball with Randy Johnson. Your mind wants you to keep living, so it advises you against making these, as well as many other, stupid decisions. The problem with many fears players face in hockey is the validity of the fear. Put the fear in perspective. You're not going to die if you make a mistake, get hit by someone bigger than you, or miss a defensive assignment. Having fear on your mind this way will only undermine your game. So first your must recognize the emotion. You can feel it in the present, but all fears exist because you're thinking about a future situation. Don't resist the fear or try to tell yourself it's not there. This will just make the fear stronger and further undermine your performance. Instead, realize it's a natural emotion, everyone feels it, including your teammate sitting next to you. Pinpoint what the fear is and turn it into an action-oriented challenge. The fear is causing the fight or flight response in your body, so you can use the chemicals such as adrenaline to your advantage. (If you're afraid of getting hit by someone bigger than you, hit him first. Then you'll see it's no big deal and the fear is gone. You can run from fear, or you can get angry and attack it.)

Jack Dempsey
"The Manassa Mauler"

In an excerpt from *The Toughest Men in Sports,* Jack Dempsey is described as this:

If ever there was a man born to fight, it was Jack Dempsey. Entering the world on June 24, 1895, in a small town called Manassa, Colorado, he stormed through the boxing ranks in a style that had never been seen before and has not been duplicated since. He earned his fighting spurs in the rough mining towns of the West, and fought for peanuts. He would take on anyone, anytime, anywhere, for just about any price. If he lost he would go hungry. He would ride the railways like a hobo and get off at a saloon looking for a fight. At 160 lbs. he would walk through the doors and announce "I can't dance and I can't sing, but I'll lick anyone in the house." According to legend, he never lost a fight.

After knocking out a fighter, 85 pounds bigger than him, a trainer by the name of Jack "Doc" Kearns took notice. He brought Dempsey up through the ranks including fighting six times in 1919 for a total of 8 rounds. That year would lead him to the World Heavyweight Boxing Championship. Jack Dempsey, known as the Savage Beast, fought a title fight against Jess Willard in 1919 in 110 degree heat of Toledo, Ohio. Dempsey was 5 inches shorter than the 6'6" Willard and weighed 70 pounds less. Dempsey later said, "When I climbed into the ring and looked across at him (Willard), I damned near fainted. He looked tremendous. I looked up at Willard and felt scared. Scared enough to have grabbed my robe and run out of the ring---if I dared." But instead he trusted his training and used his fear to his advantage. Dempsey started the fight slowly, not charging across the ring in his customary style. And then he exploded out of his shell. According to one writer that was there "He charged forward........and shot a wilting right to the ribs, then swung the left hook that poets should write about. It hit Willard in the jaw and broke it in seven places. Willard went down, got up and, with Dempsey standing over him, was smashed down again. The next time he got up, Dempsey tore in, hitting body, jaw, eye, mouth. Willard went down seven times, and the last time---four teeth missing, jaw broken, eye closed, bleeding from the nose—he could not get up. He won the fight and the title. He defended the title 5 times successfully, always against fighters much bigger then he was.

If one of the toughest men every to enter the ring in boxing had feelings of fear then you know you're not alone.

If the fear has to do with making mistakes in a big game then use routines-which are very important and you will learn later in the book- and breathing to stay in the present. While in the present you can trust and rely on your physical skills to get you through it. Once the action starts and your blood starts pumping, the fear will melt away. Remember in order to accomplish anything in life you have to ACT. Michael Jordan calls fear an illusion. As far as you're concerned you want more than anything that puck on your stick in the last minute.

Finally ask yourself these questions. How does fear limit your true potential in hockey? What are your most common fears? Will these fears help or hurt you 10 games from now, 50 games, 1 year, 5 years?

Jealousy:

Mickey Mantle: Roger, are we feuding?
Roger Maris: They said so on TV, it must be true.
Mickey Mantle: Well f*** you then.
Roger Maris: Up yours

This is taken from the movie 61* (2001) documenting teammates Roger Maris and Mickey Mantle relationship while chasing Babe Ruth's home run record. They competitively pushed each other throughout the season and Roger Maris ultimately ended up breaking the single season home run record.

To me, hockey is the ultimate team sport. I've been involved with a number of different sports, and I've never felt closer to a group of people than I did on long bus trips with the team after a great win. Our lives are defined by the friends we've met through the teams we've been lucky enough to play on. But in saying this I've known a number of players that quietly hope another fails. It's not exactly that we want them to crash and burn "top gun style", but instead hope we stay just ahead of them in points or whatever yardstick being used to track performance. This went on quite a bit when I played over five years ago. And looking in from the outside today, I can tell that it's become even more competitive between fellow players fighting for the same junior, college, and pro spots.

Let's lay it all out there. It would be great to be the best, and I hope you read this book with that goal in mind. I also understand that it is only human nature to compare yourself with other players and measure your own achievements against them. However this doesn't help the team or yourself. If you feel a twinge of jealousy when a teammate scores, then it will severely affect your game and ultimately undermine the team. The term "cancer" will be used to describe you and it's a very tough label to shed. Plus, if you choose to measure everything you do against someone on your own team, then you will always pace yourself against that player. And trust me, that player isn't the best around. However the worst part is losing focus of your own game and getting wrapped up in chasing his. It's not a good situation to put yourself in.

Start by realizing these feelings are only natural. You play hockey, so you're likely to be extremely competitive. Being competitive is not the problem. It's a trait all great players share. Recognize the feelings and also be happy for your teammate, yet use it as a positive challenge to motivate yourself. In reality, the better a teammate performs the more it helps you. If you're on his line then you're benefiting from his play. With both of you playing great, the team will go further. This attracts more scouts and brings more opportunities. Don't beat yourself up if you have these feelings. It's great to want to be the best but don't be prideful either.

Frustration:

Tommy: Forget it, I quit, I can't do this anymore, man. My head's about to explode. My whole life sucks! I don't know what I'm doing, I don't know where I'm going. My dad just died, we just killed Bambi, I'm out here getting my a$$ kicked and every time I drive down the road I wanna jerk the wheel into a Goddamn bridge abutment! --- Tommy Boy (1995)

Frustration is a close cousin to the above feeling of anger. A lot of times frustration brings on anger and then also repeated failed attempts can cause small amounts of anger which in turn brings on frustration. If you can't control the anger and you feel things are staying the same or getting worse, then you become frustrated. It's an individual response, but in hockey it can quickly spread through the entire team. Have you ever seen the most talented player on your favorite NHL team get into a fight? He's "mad as hell and not going to take it anymore." That fight is the tipping point, but if you go back and analyze his preceding shift or game you will notice he wasn't playing well. For whatever reason, something happened—probably more than twice-- that angered him and at this point he couldn't control his emotions spiraling out of control. His frustration level peaked and he took himself out of the game. Maybe the other team was shadowing him or things simply weren't going his way. This caused the reaction you saw. Opposing coaches and players know a hothead and will purposely take "cheap shots" early in the game. It's a tactic that has worked and will continue to work if you don't know how to control the frustration you feel. The main thing is to recognize the emotion. Yes, someone or something isn't going your way or even at all fair *(the ref, fans, any number of circumstances seem to be going against you).* This will cause the anger and the continued frustration. Then use the deep breathing exercise from the anger section earlier. This will calm you down and let you get back to your original game plan that you prepared for all day. You can't play well while feeling frustrated, but if you work through it, the tide will eventually begin to turn. It becomes a challenge. **You and your team against the world.** It can and will be overcome which will lead to a flood of positive emotions, including confidence. You must control your emotions or they will control you. Sound Familiar?

Defeated (Depression):

Fred Jung: Sometimes you're flush and sometimes you're bust, and when you're up, it's never as good as it seems, and when you're down, you never think you'll be up again, but life goes on. ----Blow (2001)

This can be the most debilitating mind set for any player. It literally zaps energy from your body and makes coming to the rink a chore rather than a privilege. This defeatism or depression that affects players and teams consists of a string of bad events that can't seem to be escaped. It's getting accustomed to losing and almost expecting it that pervades many teams and individuals. Picture these scenarios. There's five minutes left in the game, you're up by two goals and all you can think of is a way to lose. Or you've gone through a slump and haven't scored in 10 games and you know that there's no way your going to score tonight. And sure enough the team gives up 3 last minute goals for the loss and you definitely don't score. Then you think to yourself "see I told you it would happen. We just can't win or I will never score again." Once you reach the bottom of this well it's very hard to climb back out. I mean, why would you practice if nothing you do works? You can play angry, frustrated, or a little fearful but there's no way you can play if you've already lost in your mind before the game even begins. This emotion is a little harder to pinpoint or actually feel until it's too late. It seems to sneak up on you due to it gradually happening over a long period of time. The trick then is to consciously realize that you go through ups and downs not only in hockey, but literally every facet of your life. When you're down it's never as bad as it seems. In fact you likely won't even remember it two years from now.

The only way to get through it is by hard work and an understanding that things will change for the better. A Nike commercial from a few years ago with Dwyane Wade put this in perspective. In it he falls down 7 times while attempting a dunk but on the 8th he slams it home. It's called "Fall down 7 times, Get up 8." Never quit and find something positive-which there always is-to rally around.

ANCHORING

"Everywhere I look reminds me of her" Frank Dreblin from Naked Gun: from Files of Police Squad (1988) as he looks at the twin nuclear power plants.

What's the first thing that comes to your mind in these scenarios?

1. The sight of a cop car pulling up behind you with the lights flashing.
2. The smell of a campfire.
3. The smell of cheap tequila (for those of you old enough to drink).
4. The smell of Thanksgiving dinner.

All of the above situations mean different things to different people. The smell of a campfire for instance might bring back memories of a family trip to the lake or a bush party that was awesome. But to a firefighter, it means danger and gets the adrenaline pumping. The brain works by grouping information together. The more intense an experience was, the stronger you will feel when you recall it. You may have heard of the Russian Scientist, Ivan Pavlov, who rang a bell to get the dogs to salivate. The same thing works when you BBQ a steak around me. I can't control it. I hover over the grill to watch them cook, eating little pieces off the end. Absolutely love it.

Your past experiences have a profound effect on your present and future emotional state. The thing (sight, sound, smell, touch, taste) that brings back old memories is called an anchor. Something as simple as hearing an old song (anchor) can bring your body to the same emotional state as the situation when you won a championship and that song was playing. Or eating at a restaurant that you used to go to all the time with your ex flame. These bring back a flood of emotions from the past. How can this affect your game you ask? Take these following game situations.

1. Someone runs your goalie.
2. The goalie is out of position and you miss the wide open net.
3. Someone cross checks you from behind into the boards.
4. The coach doesn't play you for the entire first period.

What do you feel in a game when these situations happen?

As I write these I can even feel my anger boiling up. The problem is that you can't play hockey in this emotional state. You lose focus and do something stupid or worst yet take yourself out of the entire game. In these situations your emotions control you. It's like being up sh**t creek without a paddle. Whether you like it or not the current is going to take you over the falls.

The trick that many powerful people use to control these negative emotions is called anchoring. It's essentially the paddle to steer you clear of the emotional falls. You develop an anchor-usually touch-based because you can easily do it during a game-by first putting yourself in a positive emotional state. Replay the greatest moment of your career in your mind, and at your peak feeling you create a unique anchor *(biting your thumbnail, making a tight fist with your hand, interlocking your pinkies and pulling, etc).* After repeating this over and over in that peak emotional state, these emotions will be anchored to that peak feeling. This will help you stay in your optimal emotional state.

How to Anchor:

1. Remember a time during a hockey game when everything went right. Everything you touched went in the net, you hit someone harder than ever before, or you stopped every shot you faced. What is the number one play on your career highlight reel?
2. When you **relive this play and every emotion associated with it (go back to the visualization section if you need help with this)**, then do something unique with your hands (for example, bring the thumb and forefinger together, touch your ear, make a tight fist) and you will anchor the experience.
3. **Recall**, or imagine several other **similar plays** to strengthen the feeling you desire while applying the anchor developed above.
4. **Test** the anchor in practice by doing it in between drills. It should bring on the same feeling of confidence that you felt when visualizing your best plays.

In the above scenario we use the feeling of touch to anchor certain feelings of confidence. You can also use a sound (you may already do this with certain songs from your iPod) or a mental picture (I personally used the mental picture of 6 am workouts for reaching deep in 3rd period situations when I was tired) to strengthen the feeling.

For example let's say you miss an open net and start to get down on yourself. As you recognize the negative emotion on the bench, stop your thoughts and simply fire the anchor that you have associated with confidence or another positive emotion. This immediately changes your state from negative back to positive and allows you to play the rest of the game with confidence. If you get another opportunity to make the twine bulge you won't be thinking-"here we go again". Instead you will be ready with confidence to bury it and get on the score sheet.

Summary of Controlling Your Emotions Chapter

- Hockey is a very stressful sport. Your body goes through physical and mental changes that can negatively affect your game if you don't recognize your emotions. Stress can be used to your advantage in certain situations but if you let it spiral out of control the side effects prevent you from playing up to your full potential.

The most common emotions that can sidetrack your game include:

1. **Anger**—This is perhaps the most common emotion felt on the ice. First, recognize the emotion. Then, either calm yourself down using breathing exercise or use it as a motivational tool.
2. **Fear (F.** alse **E.** vidence **A.** ppearing **R.** eal**)** —This isn't an emotion that hockey players readily admit to having, but as shown with the heavyweight boxing champion Jack Dempsey, it's common for everyone to feel it at some point. You can choose to eliminate or use it to your advantage—"feel the fear and do it anyway."
3. **Jealousy**—We all want to be the greatest player around. It's the competitive spirit in us. That's not the issue. Feeling anything but joy and happiness when a teammate scores however is an issue. Realize that the greater success a teammate has the better the team becomes and the better you look. There's enough success for everyone on a good team.
4. **Frustration**--If you can't control the anger and you feel circumstances getting worse then you become frustrated. Playing frustrated is like skating around the ice with blinders on. Not helpful. Simply recognize the emotion and use the frustrating circumstances as a challenge.
5. **Defeated**—Defeatism is the worst funk a hockey player

can fall into. All the above emotions can be turned around and used as a positive force but defeatism drags you down and spreads very quickly throughout a team. The only way to get through it is with hard work, determination, and a positive outlook.

Anchoring--Your past experiences have a tremendous effect on your current emotional state. You can develop a quick and easy way to experience a positive emotional state from the past by anchoring.

Stretching

Stretching Section

I used to fear the sit and reach test. The stupid box—which I always thought my gym teacher made in his garage--was pulled out twice a year in middle school. I would sit with my legs straight and reach as far as my chubby body could take me. Even if I cheated with a little knee bend I still couldn't come close to my toes. Then they would reset the sliding ticker so you could push again. I would get as far as maybe my knees the second time. This was the only test holding me back from getting the national merit of fitness award. (As a fat kid I had to really push myself on the pull-ups too.) It was absolutely devastating.

Even with dedicating my winter to hockey and my summers to baseball, I never gave stretching much thought. At the time, most hockey players I knew avoided stretching like a Christmas Break bag skate. Everyone was more concerned with adding a couple of mph's to their slapshot, perfecting the rarely used hip check, or developing the highest saucer possible. Let the goalies worry about stretching and their weird obsession for doing the splits. Forwards and Defensemen should worry about puck control and skating. (*Little did I know at the time that both puck control and skating have a great deal to do with stretching.)*

Recently along with advances in weightlifting, cardio training, and mental preparation, stretching has become a focal point of professional athletes in all sports. Many of the best players have begun to incorporate yoga into their daily workouts. This just goes to show the importance of flexibility, which is defined as the ability to move muscles and joints through their full range of motions. Stretching will improve the body's balance, extend the range of lower body motion needed for skating, and also prevent injuries. Think about how many times you've seen a player fall awkwardly with his leg bent back up around his head. This highlight makes you cringe and simultaneously move away from the TV all in one motion. A collision like this would cause an average person's muscles to literally snap off the bone. But the pros get right back up and ask for more next shift. This is due to the muscles' pliability developed through repeated stretching and a good warm-up before the game.

As a kid, your parents would get you to the rink 30 minutes before a game with barely enough time to get dressed in a freezing cold locker room. There wasn't much time to mix in a warm-up or any sort of a stretch prior to hitting the ice. In my experience, stretching was first introduced by wasting extremely expensive ice time sitting in a circle at center ice before practice in a quick team stretch led by the captain or coach. As you got older the team would go through a "token" stretch in the hallway before the game/practice. However, this time was used more for chirping your teammates than loosening up muscles. Stretching was never looked upon as a potential benefit to a player's game. It was only viewed as a way to prevent injuries.

There are 206 bones in the body and over 600 muscles. Dedicated stretching will improve a player's ability to learn and perform skilled movements, enhance development of body awareness, and reduce risk of injury to joints, tendons, and muscles. It elongates the muscle fibers and connective tissues to improve range of motion around a joint. A warm and stretched muscle is elastic and stretchable and will work quickly. A cold, tight muscle will restrict your movement and is more easily injured. The intense workout of hockey forces nearly every muscle through its full range of motion. The greater range you have, the better you're able to perform. For that smooth, coordinated movement that great players use to make skating seem effortless, you need the muscles to stretch and contract to a great degree. This cannot happen without a dedicated stretching program both before and after every game and practice. It is said that elite athletes should stretch 1-2 times a day, 5-7 days a week. In doing so you can use 4 different stretching methods:

1. **Static Flexibility**—relates to range of motion about a joint with a stretch and hold process. Each stretch focuses on an specific muscle area. This is the most common form of stretching used today. (And it's used all wrong as

you'll see below.) An example of this is your current team stretch, in which you sit or stand around stretching each muscle. This type of stretching should be done after the athlete is warm.

2. Ballistic Stretching---this stretch involves bouncing through the stretch. By using the force of your body weight, you can stretch the muscle further than the static flexibility method. An example of this is bouncing up and down to try and touch your toes. The bouncing brings your further down each time. This type of stretching can cause soreness and injury. I'm sure you've been warned about this type of stretch by every gym teacher and coach as far back as you can remember. Although when done properly this method has its merits, we stay away from it in this book.

3. Dynamic Stretching—this type of stretching involves performing a physical exercise (25-65% of your max) while going through the same type of motions as you do on the ice. An example of this is high knee runs or the spider crawl. This is the primary way of pre-activity stretching advocated by the top trainers throughout the world. And what we focus on in the book.

5. **Active Stretching**—this involves doing a variety of active exercises with a partner or with the aid of an object such as a towel to bring your muscles through a range of motions. An example of this is doing a partner hamstring stretch or using a towel to pull the muscle further during a stretch.

Misconceptions and truths that you may have heard about stretching:

- Research has proven that flexibility does not exist as a general characteristic but is specific to a particular joint and joint action. (Merni et al. 1981) For instance you might have very flexible hamstrings but yet the muscles in your back are really tight.
- Flexibility is related to specific sports. For instance many hockey players spend a great deal of time stretching out their quads, groins, and hamstrings but barely any time at all on the hip adductors. This is one of the main reasons for the increasing number of hip muscle injuries, which can severely shorten your season and even end your career.
- Flexibility is developed when muscles are stretched through regular and frequent exercises. This means that you need to stretch regularly (as mentioned above, elite level athletes stretch 1-2 times a day, 5-7 days a week) in order to gain the benefits.
- Flexibility is diminished when an athlete takes time off from regular stretching. This means that you if you take the summer off from stretching, your flexibility is going to suffer. Then it's back to square one, you lazy bum.
- Stretching can help you relax mentally and physically. For instance, after a tough game you can stretch instead of smashing your stick off the concrete wall to forget about your mistakes.
- Muscle fibers responsible for elongation can be stretched to over 150% of the resting state. In theory--without limitation from injury—any athlete can do the splits. This means no more excuses for failing the sit and reach test.

I'm sure you currently have a stretching routine that you go through before every game, practice, and workout. Many of the stretches and exercises highlighted below will be similar, if not the same. Other stretches will be completely new to you. I noted before, an athlete should amplify his strengths and keep his weaknesses at a baseline. Very true in most areas, but in stretching you want to be completely stretched before every physical activity. This includes spending more time on certain muscles in the body that may be tight for whatever reason. Also keep in mind that everything in hockey starts with a strong lower body and midsection. Muscles will shorten when not used to their full extent, and with hockey being a bent leg activity, the hamstrings are rarely stretched to their full extent. Over time, this may lead to back injuries or groin pulls. Conversely, improving flexibility at the hips, groin, hamstrings, and thighs will prevent injury and improve skating speed and footwork. For instance if your hip flexors are tight you won't be able to get into the 90 degree deep seated position needed for a long smooth stride. Instead a short choppy stride will become habit for you.

In this book I discuss the dynamic warm-up which is crucial before every game. I have over 40 static stretches that can be accessed at www.score100goals.com/stretches.html (It was way to long and boring to list everyone in the book.)

Dynamic Warm-up

I was doing it all wrong my whole career. Before every workout, practice, and game of my life, I went through a number of static stretches to loosen up the muscles. More often than not I was pressed for time and went through a quick static stretching routine of the large muscles such as the hamstring and quadriceps on the ice without a warm-up. **Wrong**. Science has found a better way. In fact, according to a study by the University of Nevada, Las Vegas, using static stretching *alone* before a workout will actually hurt your performance. *(I'm glad I found this out 8 years after I stopped playing.)* A good warm-up begins with getting a little sweat going and increasing blood flow to your joints and tendons which will make them more receptive before beginning the exercises. The reasoning behind the switch from static stretching to dynamic stretching to get the muscles ready for the ice is that muscles are more pliable and will react better, with limited negative consequences, when warm.

Start with an aerobic activity for 3-5 minutes that warms up your body yet doesn't tire you out for the game. Some ways to accomplish this include the following:

1. A light jog in the hallways or outside
2. Running the stairs
3. Jumping rope
4. Good old jumping jacks
5. Riding the bike

Keep it about 40-60% of your max speed. When you feel warm and have a little sweat going, then take your body through a combination of the following dynamic exercises:

Running High Knees

1. Find a long hallway or go outside the rink so that you can run at least 20 yards.
2. Run at 60% of your maximum speed. Take an exaggerated high step to drive your knee as high as possible while pushing off the toes of the foot planted on the ground.
3. Make sure to keep your arms bent at a 90 degree angle.
4. Try to get as many touches as possible with the ground over the length of the run.

Running Butt Kicks

1. Find a long hallway or go outside the rink so that you can run for at least 20 yards.
2. Use your regular running stride but exaggerate the back kick so the heel of each foot hits your butt.
3. Lean forward slightly as you run to compensate for the back kicking. Also make sure to maintain a quick, yet shallow, arm swing by driving your hands from front hip pocket to chest.
4. Run the 20 yards there and back at least 2 times.

High Knee Skips

1. Find a long hallway or go outside the rink so that you can skip at least 20 yards.
2. Drive off the balls of your feet in a skipping motion, but instead of moving forward when you skip you want to jump as high vertically as possible.
3. Your arms are bent in a 90 degree angle. When you drive your left leg up to jump vertically in the skipping motion, swing your right arm up. (The thumb should come up near

the chin.) And vice versa on the left leg. It's not a race. Every skip you want to jump as vertically high as you possible can.

Side Shuffle

1. Find a long hallway or go outside the rink so that you can shuffle for at least 20 yards.
2. Face sideways and drop your hips so that you're in a 90 degree bent knee position. Keep your chest up.
3. While keeping your toes, hips and shoulders square you want to shuffle with quick feet.
4. Make sure to stay low and don't cross-over.

Carioca

1. Find a long hallway or go outside the rink so that you can carioca-not sure where this name came from--for at least 20 yards.
2. Rotate your hips so the back foot cross-steps in front of the lead foot. Plant the feet and then take that same foot

and cross behind the other foot. (If this is confusing ask a teammate. At least one person on your team knows how to do this. Trust me.)

3. Rotate your hips and feet as quickly as possible.

Jogging Arm Circles

1. Find a long hallway or go outside the rink so that you can jog at least 20 yards.
2. Jog while making big circles in the same direction with both arms. On the way down make forward circles.
3. On the way back make backward circles. The circles should be as big as possible to really activate the shoulder muscles.

Jogging Side-to-Side/Up-Down Arm Movements

1. Find a long hallway or go outside the rink so that you can jog at least 20 yards.
2. Jog while swinging your slightly bent arms in a criss-crossing motion over your chest.

3. On the way back swing your arms up and down so that your thumbs are brushing the sides of your hips.

Knee Drives

1. Find a wall and stand about 2-3 feet away with your shoulders square. Place your arms on the wall at shoulder height. (It should look like you're going to push down the wall.)
2. Walk your feet back until you have enough room to drive your knee forward and up to your chest without coming close to the wall.
3. Start with the right leg. Really drive off the balls of your feet and explode that knee up to your chest. Repeat 10 times then change legs.

Wall Kicks Side to Side

1. Find a wall and stand about 2-3 feet away with your shoulders square to the wall. Place your arms on the wall at shoulder height. (It should look like you're going to

push down the wall.)

2. Let your left leg hand freely in front of your body. Swing your leg in a pendulum motion. Raise it as high as possible when swinging away from the body. As your leg goes up, rotate your toe slightly out and away from the body.
3. Repeat 10 times with your left leg and then switch to your right leg.

Wall Kicks Front to Back

1. Find a wall and stand about 2-3 feet away. Turn sideways. Reach out your right arm and place it on the wall about shoulder height.
2. Keep your right leg slightly bent and kick forward as high as you can. Swing the leg back through and behind your body.
3. Kick 10 times then switch legs.

Back Pedal

1. Find a long hallway or go outside the rink so that you can backpedal at least 20 yards.
2. Drop your hips. Really reach back with long strides and pump your arms through. Do this at about 60% of max speed.

Ankle Flips

1. Find a long hallway or go outside the rink so that you have enough room to do this exercise for at least 20 yards.
2. Stand straight up with your legs slightly bent. Your feet should be less than shoulder width apart.
3. Explode vertically into the air, pushing from your toes and the balls of your feet.
4. When you're in the air bring your toes up so they are pointed toward the ceiling.
5. Get them level before landing. Repeat over the 20 yard distance.

Spiderman

1. Find a hallway or go outside the rink so that you have enough room to crawl/walk for 20 yards.
2. Drop down in pushup position. Bring your right leg up and place it just above and to the side of your right hand on the ground. At the same time you're going to reach up with the left arm.
3. Stretch your right hand so it's past your left hand. (You kinda walk forward with your hands.) Drag your left toe along the ground and then bring your left foot higher than your left hand.
4. Keep your hips low to the ground. Don't raise your butt in the air.

Walking Lunge

1. Find a hallway or go outside the rink so that you have enough room to perform the walking lunge for 20 yards.
2. Drive your knee up toward your chest. Then step out far enough so that the knee does not come over the toe. It

should be straight up over the ankle. Keep your chest in an upright position.

3. Then take the back leg and drive it up into your chest as you move forward.
4. Perform this walking lunge over the entire 20 yards.

Scorpions

1. This exercise is done lying on the ground but you must have enough room to kick your legs fully to the side.
2. Lay on your stomach with your arms straight out.
3. Swing your left leg over your right leg. Try to touch your right hand with your left toes.
4. Then swing your right leg over your left leg. Try to touch your left hand with your right toes.
5. Do 5 leg swings with each leg

Ok. That's 15 dynamic warm-up exercises that are well-matched for hockey. (There are many more if you do a search on Google.) You don't want to do all 15. Even if you fly through each drill without taking the time and care to do it right, it's still going to be too long. Try all of the exercises over the course of a few games and practices. Take the best 8-10 and use them before every workout, practice, and game. This will get your muscles prepared for the intense work situations ahead. Remember the 5 minute aerobic warm-up to raise your body temperature and get a little sweat going before getting into the dynamic warm-up.

Summary of Stretching Section Chapter

- Dedicated stretching improves the body's balance, extends the muscles range of motion, prevents injury, promotes clear mental thinking, and will overall improve your game.

- Warm-up for 5 minutes before the dynamic stretching to get a little sweat going.

- Perform the dynamic stretches at 60% of regular speed.

There are 4 different stretching methods but this book only focuses on the dynamic warm-up. 25 pages of Static and Active Stretching can be found at:
www.score100goals.com/stretching.html

1. **Dynamic Stretching**—this type of stretching involves performing a physical exercise (25-65% of your max) while going through the same type of motions as you do on the ice. Optimally done to get a sweat going and loosen muscles before an exercise.

Pick 8-10 of the dynamic warm-ups exercises and use them before every game. Make sure you get the upper body involved too.

Games

Games

You could hear a pin drop on the bus ride to the rink. Everyone was lost in their own thoughts, mentally preparing. We were representing the USA at the 2000 World Junior tournament on our way to the Semifinal game against the Czech Republic in Umea, Sweden. The entire hockey world, from NHL players, scouts, friends, and family were going to be watching. Heck, even Don Cherry was probably watching with a pen and paper ready to turn any mistake into a segment on Hockey night in Canada. Without a doubt it was the biggest game of our lives. The bus stopped and we walked single file out the door, through the fans waiting in the freezing cold outside the rink and the hundreds of huddled scouts trading notes on the players from the early game still on the ice. Not a word was said as we made our way to the locker room. The trainers had been working all day to get our equipment prepared and now it was our time to get prepared mentally and physically. Preparedness was the key to success. This was pounded into us all camp. The stretch was in half an hour so we all went about our separate routines around the locker room.

In order to stretch as a team we needed to go to a huge lobby area. As the team made our way through the lobby we had to pass the Czech team that was also getting prepared. Even though things have changed since the 80s we expected a bunch of serious soldier like players with deadpan faces. But instead of a team stretch like us, these guys were playing soccer and laughing their butts off. 1, 2, 3, 4…… the Czech team repeatedly chanted in their language as they tried to juggle a soccer ball in the air for our entire team stretch. Needless to say their pre-game routine was on the opposite end of the spectrum then ours. And it seemed to work on that occasion. They shut us down 4-1 in a game where we could barely breathe let alone score because their checking was so tight.

No pre-game routine is right or wrong, but since this

tournament, my eyes were opened to a completely different preparation routine. The quiet, introspective, get serious pre-game that I had come to use my whole life is good for some people preparing for a game. I couldn't imagine Scott Stevens getting ready to freight train people by playing hacky-sack in the hallway like my hippie friend Charlie, but the game of hockey is supposed to be fun. Why not add a little bit of that to the pre-game? If anything, it will loosen you up. So here are a few ways to warm up while having some fun and also develop some useful game skills.

Feet and Concentration

Soccer Drills

"During warm-ups I kick the ball, pass it under one foot and then the other, bring it up. I do it out of sheer pleasure but also to relieve stress. It's my way of relaxing, of reducing the pressure of the game, of calming myself down. I don't like to think a lot before a match. Playing around with the ball works as a perfect antidote, neutralizing all the worries and enabling me to concentrate."-----CRISTIANO RONALDO, Manchester United player of the year

I know that if you play hockey and you're from anywhere in North America, then you're probably not very familiar with the world's most popular game. I agree. You can't use your hands, any innocent shove is penalized, and 3 to 5 times a game players flop around like fish on a boat deck. Not cool. But sharing the hallways in an international tournament showed me that pretty much all the Europeans warm-up before every game with a soccer ball. They compete in a bunch of different games that have hockey specific conditions. It lightens the mood and more importantly heightens the body's coordination and the mind's focus.

Juggling

What you need to start: Grab a soccer ball and form a circle with 5 to 10 players.

The object of the game: Keep the ball in the air using anything but your hands.

How it works: The players stand in a circle and try to juggle the ball in the air using anything but their hands. A player is eliminated from the circle for that particular round when he makes a mistake and the ball touches the ground. (Judgment calls here. Say for instance someone kicks the ball a million mph off someone else's head, then the player who kicked it is out.) The last player standing wins the round. You can play a different variation where you only keep it in the air with your head or you have to hit it a least twice before putting it back in play. It's a fun game that strengthens your coordination and gets the competitive juices flowing before the real game. (If you watch the pre-game interviews and preparations for NHL games, the background usually shows players kicking the soccer ball around in this game.)

Pepper

What you need to start: Grab a soccer ball and have 3-4 players stand shoulder to shoulder in a line and 1 player stands on the triangular point 5 feet away.

The object of the game: One time the ball through passes back and forth to get the feet moving and a little sweat going.

How it works: This is a baseball game used to develop quick hands before a game. We use the soccer ball to develop quick feet. The game starts with one player from the line kicking the ball to the lone player on the point. The player on the point has to one time it back to any of the other players in line. Whoever receives the ball one times it back to the point man. This back and forth passing continues for at least 10 repetitions, and then one player from the line moves to the point position. All the players rotate through. It's a lot harder than it sounds-move further away from each other to increase the difficulty- to control the ball and will definitely get the heartbeat up and feet moving. It's a great warm-up drill.

Catch

What you need to start: Grab a soccer ball and another teammate. You need a long hallway or you can go outside the rink.

The object of the game: Passing the soccer ball over increasing distance. Kicking the soccer ball back and forth will warm up your feet and get you focused.

How it works: Have you ever been to a baseball game before the first pitch? The players play catch back and forth on a rope over half the field. They warm up their arms at increasing distances for at least 15 minutes. In hockey terms, passing the puck back and forth with your feet stationary doesn't really warm up your hands or your feet. And besides, ice time is freaking expensive. The soccer ball allows you to pass it back and forth and run around a little. Grab a teammate and start about 10 feet apart. Kick the ball between each other for a couple of minutes then double the distance. Kick it another couple of minutes then double the distance between each other again. Besides running around chasing the ball to get a sweat going, kicking over a long distance forces you to concentrate on making accurate passes which directly translates to the game.

Stairs

Many pro hockey players run up the arena stairs before actually suiting up. This warms up their coordination abilities and gets a good sweat going. In fact, as a spectator if you can skip the tailgating or pre-game bratwursts and get into a stadium before any sport, you will see a number of players running the stairs. Yeah, I know what you're thinking. Not really a fun game. It actually kind of sucks, but the pros believe that it helps their game, so give it a try. There are a couple of different patterns to not only break a sweat and get your feet moving, but also to coordinate your brain activity with your feet. This is definitely needed after a pre-game nap. Also the game ahead requires your legs to respond with explosive movements that running the stairs will condition. So hook up your iPod and strap on the running shoes.

(**Always walk back down the stairs. By running down the stairs you must absorb 7 to 12 times your body weight with each step. That's a lot of pressure and impact stress on your knees. Don't risk the injury. *****)**

Normal Climb

What you need to start: One section of arena stairs that go straight up.

The object of the game: Get adjusted to running the stairs. This exercise will get the blood flowing and quickly get you warmed up for the following more complicated stair exercises.

How it works: Start by running up the stairs at 50% max. The pattern is the same as you would normally walk up the stairs. Hit each step with one foot. Next time run up the stairs 75%. Do this only one time at each different speed.

Touch every stair

What you need to start: One section of arena stairs that go straight up.

The object of the game: This exercise develops quick feet and gets a good sweat going.

How it works: Run up the stairs at around 50%-75% of your max speed. Any faster could result in injury and drain your energy before the game. Touch each stair with both feet. Start by stepping up to the first stair with left or right foot, then follow with your opposite foot. Move on to the next stair with your starting foot. It doesn't matter which foot you start with as long as you move to the next stair with the same foot each time. Continue this pattern to the top of the stairs. Walk down. Repeat 1 time.

Switch Feet

What you need to start: One section of arena stairs that go straight up.

The object of the game: Warm-up the central nervous system and coordinate the feet with the brain.

How it works: Run up the stairs at around 50%-75% of your max speed. Just as before this exercise consists of touching each step with both feet, but instead of progressing up the stairs with the same foot each time you switch it up. This is easier than it sounds. Start by stepping up to the first step with your left foot. Then follow up on that same step with your right foot. Step up the next stair with the right foot. Continue up to the top always rotating the foot you step up to the next step with. Walk down.

****This is very tricky. In Chicago, I worked out at a gym where some of the Chicago Bulls trained during the Jordan years. This was a crucial exercise they practiced everyday due to their size and footwork needed to compete. ****

Two at a time

What you need to start: One section of arena stairs that go straight up.

The object of the game: This drill stretches out your hip flexors and warms up the quadriceps needed for skating.

How it works: Run up the stairs using 35% percent speed while skipping every other stair. Walk down. Repeat 1 more time.

The objective of running the stairs in all of the above exercises is to provide a warm-up before the game. This will be one of the first physical activities that you perform before a game to get the blood moving and coordination back up to speed. Also that pre-game meal you ate not so long ago is sitting in your stomach and keeping you tired. This activity will break you out of the funk. However, don't tire yourself out or expend more energy than necessary.

Jump Rope

Michalek did not always have the intense pre-game routine, but the knee injury in his rookie season that limited him to two NHL games in two years, and the subsequent rehabilitation, changed his approach. "I used to not do anything before a game," said Michalek. "Before the injury, I would just sit and do nothing. Since the injury . . . I don't want it to happen again. At least the injury was good for something. I do 10 minutes on the bike and 15 minutes jumping rope," said Michalek. "I like to be sweating before the game. I feel better in the first period. Everything is warmed up." This details the warm-up regime of Milan Michalek.

A few years ago they designed a survey based on the athleticism and strength needed to play every sport imaginable from hockey, soccer, basketball, crew, rugby, cricket, etc. You name it and they had it on the list. They handed this survey out to random athletes from all over the world and had them rate the difficulty of each sport. The overall consensus from the surveyed athletes' perspective is that "**only**" boxing was an all around tougher sport to play than hockey. Footwork in boxing can mean delivering a knockout blow or taking one on the chin so it's pretty critical to their workout regime. Before a game if you jump rope for ten minutes, this will quickly raise your heart rate and get your quick feet muscle memory started. Specific areas of your brain handle the motor network involved with hand to foot coordination and agility. This is already highly inherent in a hockey player but jumping rope will take you to the next level. Jumping rope serves as an excellent total body warm-up before dynamic stretching.

Skating requires great conditioning, explosiveness, ankle strength, balance, coordination, agility, speed, and quickness. Jumping rope develops all of these physical attributes for that physical edge going into the game. A jump rope is easy to travel with and convenient to use at the rink. People may look at you funny but they're actually impressed if you can nail this.

Trust me. It's an excellent way to raise the heart rate and warm up the muscles.

Regular Jumps

What you need to start: A high ceiling hallway or just go outside the rink. Plus a jump rope and a pair of running shoes.

The object of the game: Coordination, quick feet, and warming-up the muscles.

How it works: Swing the rope over your head and under your feet slowly. Just like in gym class. Start by going slowly and get the coordinated jumping motion down. Stay on the balls of your feet and jump with both feet at the same time. Gradually ramp up the pace until it's a constant jumping action as soon as your feet touch the ground.

----Do this for 2-4 minutes---

One Foot

What you need to start: A high ceiling hallway or go outside. Jump rope and running shoes.

The object of the game: This exercise is very effective for improving your coordination and developing quick feet that translates directly to the game.

How it works: Once you've developed a rhythm with the regular jump you can start jumping on one foot. Begin with either your right or left foot only for 5 consecutive jumps, then switch to the other foot for 5 consecutive jumps. After doing 5 consecutive jumps with each foot then alternate feet with each rotation of the jump rope.

---Repeat this pattern for 1-3 minutes---

High Jump

What you need to start: A high ceiling hallway or go outside. Jump rope and running shoes.

The object of the game: Develops concentration, coordination, and explosive power.

How it works: After reaching top speed with the regular jump, try to rotate the rope twice under your feet with each single jump. This takes some practice and to be honest is kind of a showboating trick. It forces you to change the height of your jump and increases your hand to feet coordination. It takes some time to learn this jumping technique so practice it before trying it in the pre-game and getting frustrated.

Backwards

What you need to start: A high ceiling hallway or venture outside. Jump rope and running shoes.

The object of the game: Improves your motor system coordination and stretches the calves, quads, and hamstrings.

How it works: Just like regular jumping with two feet at the same time except rotate the rope backwards. It's not pretty when you first try this. In fact the first 100 times or so you jump backwards the rope will most likely get tangled in your feet. Just like the double rotation explained above, practice this jump before actually integrating it into your routine.

Reaction Time and Concentration for the Hands

Tennis Ball Exercises

Bounce Back

What you need to start: It requires two people and 5 tennis balls.

The object of the game: This is primarily a goalie drill, but can also be used for forwards and defensemen to work on their reactionary skills, peripheral vision, and coordination.

How it works: One person stands about 5 feet away from the wall. The other person holding the 5 tennis balls stands a couple of feet behind at angle. (If you're a lefty move over a foot or two to the left so you can throw without hitting the player in front with the ball. Vice versa if you're a righty.) Both players are facing the wall so the player in front can't see when the player behind tosses the ball. The player in back tosses the ball at the wall so it bounces back to the player in front. The player closest to the wall needs to catch the ball before it passes him. At first, start by tossing it softly and let the player know when it's coming. Then gradually increase the speed and disguise when and where it's coming. This will force the player in front catching the ball to increase his reaction time and move laterally.

Stickhandling for Quick Hands

If you get to the John Labatt Centre early or travel on the road, you'll find Perry (Cory Perry now playing with the Anaheim Ducks) standing on the ice dressed in his black hockey underwear and shower sandals. He'll be stickhandling, doing tricks, working some magic with the stick and the puck.

"I'm in my own little world," said Perry. "I just think about the game and what I'm going to be doing that night. It's just a little quiet place. It's my time to be alone and not be bothered by anybody."

Stickhandling

This drill uses a weighted stick to warm-up the hands and wrists used for shooting and stickhandling. It's a form of deceleration training that physically and psychologically helps your stickhandling ability. This is comparable to the donut or weighted bat which has been used in baseball for over 75 years. As you have probably personally used or seen, a baseball player will either swing with a couple of bats or place a weighted donut over the bat. The idea behind this is to increase bat speed and develop the arm muscles used in hitting. Some professionals claim this can increase bat speeds by up to 8 mph. Using a weighted stick to warm up with in hockey also increases your hand speed for quick, tight moves. I had the opportunity to watch

Pierre Turgeon who was a great stickhandler warm up before games and practices while using a weighted hockey stick.

What you need to start the following exercises: You will need 2 to 6 pucks depending on your strength and skill level as well as some tape. Start by taping 2 pucks side to side on the front center of your back up stick. (As you get used to two pucks, you can tape an increasing number to the front and back of the stick. Make sure it's evenly weighted.) One tennis or golf ball.
The object of the game: With this weighted stick, use a tennis or golf ball to stickhandle for a couple of minutes. Quickly go through the following exercises with the weighted stick and ball. This will stretch and loosen up the wrists and arms as well as strengthen them.

Front of Body

How it works: Get in a hockey position with your legs shoulder width apart and knees bent. Extend your arms out from your body. Your elbows should be in front of your body, not touching your sides. (The top hand holding your stick should be in-front of your body not tucked in by your ribs.) By having your arms extended it gives you a bigger stickhandling radius with the puck and allows more room to pull the puck toward your body when a defender tries to poke check you. (Watch how Jaromir Jagr stickhandles.) Stickhandle the puck back and forth in front of your body. The width of each side to side stickhandle should be just outside both legs. Really exaggerate rolling your wrists with both the top and bottom hand. Continue this back and forth motion until you establish a rhythm and good control. Then move to stickhandling on the side of your body.

Side of Body

How it works: Get in a hockey position with your legs shoulder width apart and knees bent. Make sure to look straight ahead with your toes, hips, and shoulders square. Stickhandle front to back on the left side of your body with a width of about 3 feet.

After stickhandling on this side for about 1-2 minutes switch sides. Your backhand side will obviously be harder because it's initially an awkward position and you probably have never practiced this stickhandling motion. That's alright, just keep at it and you will improve. After you feel comfortable stickhandling on your sides then try to form a figure 8 with the puck to work on pulling the puck into the body.

Figure 8

How it works: Get into a hockey position with your legs shoulder width apart and knees bent. Stickhandle the puck in a figure 8 movement. Imagine two stationary cones a couple of feet directly in front of the toes of each foot. Start by pushing the puck up and around the imaginary cone on the outside and then pull it through the middle of the imaginary objects. (Feel free to use a couple of pucks or water bottles if you need the physical obstacle there.) This will put the puck on your backhand. Next cradle the puck on your backhand around the imaginary object in front of your other foot and then pull it back through the middle. If you were to look at this exercise from above it would look like the ball is going in a figure 8 pattern. Keep up this pattern for 1-2 minutes. This really stretches out your wrists due to the rolling action needed for pulling and cradling the puck. After this pattern try a stickhandling maneuver to develop full arm extension.

Quick 1-2 then Long

I originally learned this stickhandling move from Aleksey Nikiforov, the Russian coach I mentioned before. Aleksey coached for a youth hockey team in Russia where players like Alexei Kovalev (in my opinion one of the best stickhandlers in the game) and Darius Kasparitis learned their skills. He came over to the United States in the 90s and coached at my local rink in Riverside, Long Island. He played a big role in a number of great players entering the NHL in the past couple of years from the Long Island area including Higgins and Komiserek. Every practice Aleksey would show us one unique move that we had most likely never seen before. His goal was to teach us to think outside the box. It was his way of opening our minds to what you can do with a little creativity and practice. Then he would tool around all of us with the same move. Great fun. Although he loved the toe drag, Alexei stressed this next movement over all others. He said it's the basis for every move to beat an opposing player. It consists of stickhandling quickly just outside one foot(either right or left) then pulling the puck across the body along with a shoulder/head fake to get the defenseman leaning to that side (The more you exaggerate that fake, the more the opposing player will bite on it.), and then pushing the puck all the way to the extreme outside of the other foot. Now you have a step on the defenseman and can use your speed to bust wide around him.

How it works: To practice this, start by stickhandling a few times very quickly just outside your right or left foot. The width of the stick handling movement should be about one foot. Then pull the puck in a diagonal line across and into the body so it ends up outside of your opposite foot, turn your shoulder (the defensemen should see the back of your shoulder blade) and drop your head to that side. This provides the fake to get the defenseman leaning. Then explode laterally off that outside foot. (Think about the Heiden/Slide Board where you push from side to side) and take the puck to the far extreme of the other side of your body. In a game situation this is the exact time where you can beat a defenseman wide. But instead, in this exercise stop and stickhandle a few quick times outside of the foot you just landed on and brought the puck over to, complete your head/shoulder fake on that side of your body, then explode back laterally off that foot, and bring the puck to the other side of the body. Continue the quick stickhandling and lateral movement from side to side for about a minute. This is an unbelievable training exercise, but be careful not to tire yourself out before a game.

Toe Drag

Ahhh. It's the nastiest move in hockey, when you make a defenseman lunge for the puck as you pull it back toward your body with the toe of your stick blade. Then you bring it around to the other side of your body and blow by the stupid-looking turnstile of a defenseman. Warming up with this movement develops your reach and helps you practice pulling the puck back toward the body. This little pull back movement is used countless times throughout a game to gain control of the puck or to keep it away from a defender.

How it works: The ball starts on your forehand with your arms fully extended to the outside of that foot. Pull the puck with the toe of your stick in a half circular motion toward the closest foot. If you're looking directly down at a player from above executing the movement, it would look like a C cut in the ice, starting with your arms fully extended and bringing it into your foot. After pulling the puck back and into your body then quickly slide the puck across in front of your body. The puck will end up on your backhand. If you time it right in a game, the defenseman will lunge for the puck as you pull it back. Then you quickly cross the puck to your backhand so the defenseman will be out of position and you can blow by him. Repeat this process 5-10 times.

If you're feeling crazy, also try doing it on your backhand. Have only your top hand on the stick and that arm fully extended. Pull the ball on your backhand using just your top hand, with the toe of your stick blade in a circular motion towards your closest foot. Then immediately grab the stick with your bottom hand and slide the puck to your forehand on the furthest side of your body. Very tough to do, but I think that you should practice seemingly impossible moves to eliminate limiting beliefs and also for the creativity it develops. And if you do pull this move off and someone gets it on tape, send me the Youtube.com url. You will become a Jedi in the hockey world.

Saucer Pass (Extra fun game if you have time)

"The Sauce" consists of passing the puck in the air, so you can get it over defensemen's sticks and outstretched players, and then have it land flat on the ice.

What you need to start: If you're fortunate enough to have a free sheet of ice before warm-ups all you need is a stick, puck, and a partner.
The object of the game: This drill keeps the mood light while working on stickhandling and focus.
How it works: Similar to the baseball warm-up where you concentrate on hitting the placement of your partner's glove, simply stand 15-20 feet away from each other and pass it back and forth. You can lay a stick flat or use a glove as a barrier between each other. The game revolves around saucing the puck as high as possible and making it land flat on target. When you get the puck, stickhandle a few times back and forth then sauce it back to the other person. More of a fun way to pass the time and get relaxed then anything else.

Summary of Games Section Chapter

- Many players in the NHL get prepared using games and activities that are fun and develop skills which translate directly to the game.

Soccer Ball Drills: I first learned these warm-up drills watching European teams get ready for a game at the World Junior Tournament. Now every player in the NHL seems to do it during pre-game warm-up. The following games done with a soccer ball lighten the mood, develop coordination, and create focus.

1. Juggling
2. Pepper
3. Catch

Stairs: As I said before running the stairs is about as fun as a bag skate. However these following "drills" are used by pros in nearly every sport to get their mind-body in tune before a game and to get a light sweat going.

1. Normal Climb
2. Touch Every Stair
3. Switch Feet
4. Two at a Time

Jumping Rope: Excelling in hockey requires great conditioning, explosiveness, ankle strength, balance, coordination, agility, speed, and quickness. Jumping rope develops all of these for the physical edge going into the game. Boxers use this as their main conditioning tool to develop the quick feet needed to move around the ring.

1. Regular Jumps
2. One Foot
3. High Jump
4. Backwards

Tennis Ball Drill: This single drill develops lightning fast reflexes. Originally meant for goaltenders, everyone can use this to sharpen their cat like reflexes.

1. Bounce Back

Stickhandling: Use a weighted stick to go through the motions of these following stickhandling patterns. It will strengthen the wrists and arms while preparing the mind for specific game situations.

1. Front of Body
2. Side of Body
3. Figure 8
4. Quick 1-2 Then Long
5. Toe Drag

And to loosen up the mode and concentrate on hitting your passing target get on to the sheet of ice before the game and saucer pass.

Nutrition

Special Thanks to Deb Barnett a two time Olympian who wrote most of this chapter and provided a lot of the in-depth nutritional information.

Pre-game Nutrition

What are we serving tonight, chicken or... chicken?
Tommy Boy—(1995)

The hockey season is a marathon consisting of 82 sprints. It's an extremely demanding sport for which your body must be physically and mentally prepared every shift, every game. If you're lucky you get about 15-20 shifts a game. Each shift requires short bursts of speed at 100% full out intensity, with quick changes in direction and physical punishment. The anaerobic nature of a single shift lasting between 30 seconds to 1 ½ minute requires one type of energy source. The repeated expectation of this effort after 2 to 3 minute rest cycles until the completion of a one hour game demands the athlete address an aerobic energy system training as well. Also consider the mental clarity and energy required to make almost instantaneous decisions on the ice. ***YOU WILL*** short change yourself if your energy level is anything less than full. Therefore it makes common sense to pay close attention to not just your pre-game meal and hydration but also your everyday eating habits. For a hockey player to perform at his/her highest level they must understand the foundations of daily general nutrition and also performance nutrition in order to optimize fueling of the body in the best possible way.

Every hockey player needs to seriously consider their everyday nutritional habits. For most people, the nutritional foundation of balance (right amount, right time, and right variety), health (immune system, cell repair, blood lipids, blood glucose, blood pressure, liver function, blood hormones) and hydration (cell health, cell function) will be good or bad depending on their daily habits created in childhood. The elite level hockey player requires much more including performance nutrition. For performance nutrition to be most effective, good daily nutritional habits need to be maintained over the course of the season. The goal is to create a solid foundation upon which we can address fueling for elite level performance and the recovery needed from this level of exertion (e.g., performance is always limited by recovery-82 game season including practice, weight training and a long travel schedule-, scar tissue formation from constant physical play, and micro tears). The foundation of your general everyday nutritional habits provides the energy needed for the full season. The pre-game meal will maximize the energy needed to perform your best for each game.

The best long term investment you can make for your body to be fit and function at peak performance levels is to eat and especially drink in a healthy manner. Our bodies are constantly transforming energy from food into movement, activity, thought and emotion. Changing your diet into one based on high energy foods will help optimize your performance level. Focus on foods such as fresh fruit, fresh vegetables, whole grains, and fresh organic reared meat and fish. Some of the most important components of a healthy, energy full diet are: complex carbohydrates, protein, fats, fatty acids (essential), and antioxidants. (Don't worry; the book goes over this in detail throughout the chapter.)

Now the exciting part- analyzing and fine tuning your daily eating habits. Let's look at some nutritional **keys** to develop high energy as an elite level hockey player.

Key #1 HYDRATION

I'm sure you've all seen Man vs. Wild, where Bear Gylls defies death in every region of the earth. (That guy is a world class lunatic.) I have every episode on Tivo. Part of me wants to see the NASCAR crash where he battles it out with a carnivorous bear in some deep backcountry wilderness, but that's another story. While shooting an episode in the Australian outback he stated an amazing fact. He said that "humans can only survive a few hours in that heat without water." In this episode Bear goes as far as drinking his own pee for hydration. (Please don't try this at home.) But the fact of the matter is you can live around 5 weeks without food but without water a human can last only 5 days in normal circumstances. On average, the human body is about 60% water. Our brains are 70% water, our blood is 80% water and our lungs contain about 85% water. (It's hard to believe, but Dicky Dunn wrote it so it must be true.) Only oxygen is more vital to sustaining life. Throughout the day we lose water through regular perspiration, going to the bathroom, breathing, and of course perspiration by exercising. Hydration is by far the most important factor in your game preparation. If you're not properly hydrated your athletic performance will suffer. Even minor dehydration impairs contractile strength in the muscles, speed, concentration, coordination, reaction time, and stamina. Remember this, the human thirst mechanism is faulty, so waiting until you are thirsty to drink is ***TOO LATE***. Hydration must be a priority for peak performance.

TIPS:

- As a guideline try to drink 1/2oz -1oz per pound/per day.
- 190 lbs = at least 95 oz fluid per day (2.75 – 5 liters per day).
- Weigh-in before and after practices, training, and games. There shouldn't be a drastic change either in weight loss or gain. (This is especially true for goalies. I remember hearing that Glen Healy lost 14 lbs in water weight during a game in the 1993 playoffs. Not only will this effect performance during the present game but also any future games.)
- Given the nature of a hockey game with two intermissions, athletes should consume electrolytes to enhance absorption and prevent cramping. Choose a carb/electrolyte drink for 16 oz of your replacement fluids perhaps during an intermission, but then the rest of you fluid needs should be met with water. You don't need to replace all your fluids on the ice.
- Carb/electrolyte drinks- the concern with a number of the electrolyte drinks on the market is that they are a combination of non-purified water, sucrose, glucose, fructose (sugars manufactured by factories from corn) and

artificial colors with electrolytes (potassium and sodium) thrown in. More research needs to be done on the nutritional value of them. (With the explosion of new drinks onto the market including “energy drinks”, you can drop a lot of money with little to no effect. Might as well be drinking tap water.) Some feel that they do more harm than good. You can’t go wrong consuming natural mineral or spring water, fresh vegetable juice, or diluted fruit juices. But good ol’ water is still the best bet. Nothing replaces pure water for hydration. Try to get the other nutrients you need from your meals, not from marketed sugar drinks.

Pre-event	Immediately prior to event	During event	Immediately Post event	Post event recovery
1-2 hours	0-10 minutes	Drink early (6-8 oz) & at regular intervals (10-15 min.) when possible	Take in carb/protein drink (2:1 or 3:1 ratio) & banana	Re-hydrate: 20 oz per pound lost during competition. Tomato juice is good choice for part of this replacement
17-20 oz	7-10 oz		EAS - Myoplex	
Water/shake	Water/electrolytes		Nutrilite - meal replacement	
			Make your own: see recipes	

Game Day Hot Tip: Monitor your hydration level by the color of your urine. The clearer the color, the better ... if you have bright yellow urine or it has a strong smell, start pumping the fluids.

Key #2 CARBOHYDRATES

Behind hydration, complex carbohydrates are next in critical importance for athletic performance. These are found only in products made from plants. If you've ever been on a hockey bus throughout Canada or the Midwestern US, then you've seen the fields of wheat, barley, beans, and others that go into producing complex carbs. They are the major source of energy in our diets. Complex carbohydrates are made of sugar molecules linked together into long, branched chains and have beneficial effects on the way you absorb and use other nutrients. Bread, pasta, cereals, grains, fruits, and vegetables contain complex carbohydrates rich in important micronutrients of vitamins, minerals and trace elements. In terms of athletic performance, carbs provide glucose for energy before and during performance. They also provide glucose for glycogen synthesis or energy storage for any future activity. *(Be careful though too much is not a good thing. The spare tire around your waist doesn't give you nitro capabilities.)* Basically, glucose is the fuel for our body. (I told myself I would kick my own a$$ if I started using clichés, but "you are what you eat", "you can't drive a Ferrari on regular unleaded", "You can't play and train like a champion, but live like an idiot." So there you go. You've most likely heard one of these phrases and I've briefly sold out.) This includes bulky carbs in the form of fiber. Fiber is a carbohydrate that consists of very large molecules resistant to enzymatic action (which is breaking down the food into an energy source for the body.) While fiber is not digestible, it has important functions in the body. Most diets are less than 20g of fiber where a suggested 35- 40g of fiber is recommended. There are two types of fiber. (You don't have to understand the big words. Heck, I learned about them reading up and speaking with dieticians for this book, but I had to put them in here because I wanted this chapter to be both for beginners and experts.)

1. Soluble----Gums(*found in oats, seeds, legumes, and edible portions of seeds, vegetables, and fruit.)*
2. Insoluble fibers ---Cellulose and Lignins (*found in the bran of wheat*) and also Hemicellulose (*found in the whole grains of nuts, seeds, fruits, and vegetables.)* **Be careful about eating too much fiber right before a game. I ate grape nuts before the 1.5 mile run test my sophomore year in college, and it felt like I was carrying a brick around the running track in my stomach. Didn't pass the test and kept on running to the bathroom after crossing the finish line. You've been warned.)**

TIPS:

- Athletes should strive to get 55-65% of their calories from carbs (20-25 cal per pound).

- The best foods to choose are the ones least processed. In other words the fewest steps foods are removed from nature the better. Organic is a far better choice when available and the budget allows. (All kinds of grocery stores these days carry organic food. If you have a Trader Joes, Mother's Market, Whole Foods, or Henry's around your area then consider shopping there. Also most cities have a farmers' market during the week that always has fresh food. Trader Joe's is my personal favorite as it's cheap with great quality, great tasting food.)

- Look for 3g of fiber per serving or more on the label. If it DOESN'T have it, put it back and find something that does.

- Organically grown produce are preferable because pesticides and fungicides are poisonous and have a culminating effect on the body. It's nothing to lose sleep over and honestly may or may not affect your energy level come game time, but it's a good life habit to develop for future health.

- Remember: Refining and processing grains reduces nutrient values and raises their glycemic index. (This is the main reason why you have been told to eat wheat bread over white bread.)

Glycemic Index and how it Relates to Game Time Energy

Lately the buzz word within the health community has been glycemic index, due to the obesity epidemic and subsequent rise in diabetes. The glycemic properties of a food also play a major factor in your energy levels for athletic performance. The glycemic index (GI) is a measure of how fast the body turns starches into sugars. High GI foods raise blood sugar levels quickly and while this does provide a burst of energy it can be followed by a huge let down. (Think candy bar) Lower GI foods take a longer time to convert to glucose, so they maintain normal levels of blood sugar in the body and provide the energy needed at a more sustained pace. For the 2-4 hours before a game, the pre-game meal should include low glycemic foods which will provide longer sustained amounts of energy. Whereas, for energy just prior to the event (30 minutes before) and during the game, foods with a high glycemic index would be most appropriate.

Here's a listing of some common foods and their corresponding glycemic index. Start by searching for the everyday common foods you eat. *Based on their glycemic rating, do you think these foods help you maintain a steady energy level which is beneficial to your performance?* **Or do they provide quick peaks and then you come crashing down?** The healthy options in the higher GI category aren't necessarily bad and can even be used to your advantage. Gatorade and other high GI snacks such as rice cakes can be eaten 30 minutes before game time. It's critical to eat the right foods at the right time for maximum energy. Recognize these foods and avoid them early on during the game day. Take a mental note of all the foods with a low glycemic rating you like to eat or could force yourself to eat over the course of the game day.

Low Glycemic Foods	High Glycemic Foods
Breads	**Breads**
Multigrain Breads	White Bread
Wholegrain Bread	Plain Bagel
Wheat Bread	Baguette
Dark rye	
Cereal	**Cereal**
Museli	Corn Flakes
Special K	Rice Chex
All-Bran Kellogs	Cheerios
Oatmeal	Total
Snacks	**Half hour Prior to Game Snacks**
Oatmeal Cookie	(very limited amount)
Stoned Wheat Thins	Rice cakes
Banana Bread	Graham Crackers
	Pretzels

Low Glycemic Foods(cont'd)	High Glycemic Foods(cont'd)
Pre-game Meal	
Spaghetti	
Fettucine	
Linguine	
Macaroni	
(wheat options are best)	
Long White Rice	
Baked Beans	
Kidney Beans	
Soy Beans	
Tomato Sauce	
Fruit and Vegetables	**Fruits and Vegetables**
Grapes	Raisins
Kiwi	Pineapple
Apple	Watermelon
Orange	Carrots
Banana	
Broccoli	
Mushrooms	
Cauliflower	
Drinks	**Drinks**
Apple Juice	Gatorade
Orange Juice	Coke *(not even remotely a healthy option but despite this most people load up on soda all day prior to a game)*
Milk Skim – 2%	
Cranberry Juice	
Desert	
Low Fat Yogurt	

Digestion of Foods

Remember my story earlier about eating Grape Nuts cereal before a 1.5 mile run test. I know I will never forget it. This has to deal with how long it takes for the food to get broken down in your digestive track. Liquids as well as some foods get absorbed right away. Other foods are worked over by your intestinal track for hours before getting digested. If you want to feel light on your feet then eat the foods on the left side of the timeline below. If you want to feel sluggish and lethargic like you do after a Thanksgiving meal then eat the foods on the right side of the below timeline. Study this timeline and begin to develop pre-game meals and snack plans for game day.

Digestion time line:

Shortest Longest

←---→

Liquid fruits vegetables starches fats

Tips:

- The closer you get to game time means you eat items on the timeline's left side. These foods and liquids require the shortest amount of time needed for absorption through the digestive system and excretion of excess waste.

- It takes 1-4 hours for peristalsis to push food out of the stomach and into first part of small intestine. The foods on the right side of the timeline should be eaten 3-5 hours before the puck drops so enough time can elapse.

Game Day Hot Tip: Get back to grains, vegetables, and some fruit as your main source of energy versus the traditional steak and eggs pre-game meal. There's more protein in some of the grains, fruits, and vegetables than you realize.

Key #3 PROTEINS

Proteins are the building blocks of the body. They help with the growth and development of all body tissues including muscles, blood, skin, hair, nails, and internal organs. Amino acids from proteins compose most of the transmitters which relay information from the brain to the body affecting your muscular and emotional activity. This means your reaction time will be considerable slower without the proper amount of protein in your diet. Enzymes are proteins that act as catalysts for chemical reactions. Digestion, cellular energy, tissue and organ repair, and brain activity require enzymes. This is why you are ordered by your trainer to drink a protein shake after a tough workout. Pushing your body night in/night out as is required to stay on top in hockey tears down muscle. This can be seen over the course of a season as many hockey players have a tough time maintaining their weight. This weight needs to be built up or at least maintained for peak performance. Since muscle makes up most of the weight after water, it's crucial to sustain mass by eating the right amount of proteins. Society has long focused on meat as the primary source of protein; however plant foods, vegetables and grains are also good sources. Sufficient amounts of protein are critical to build, repair and maintain muscle tissue. However most people, including trainers, overstate how much protein you need as a hockey player. 07-.09 grams per pound of body weight is the highest amount of protein recommended for athletes trying to gain mass. High protein diets increase fluid loss which leads to early fatigue and dehydration. Most of the muscle and workout magazines you read tend to push the protein intake to the limit because they assume their readers are working out to look like Arnold Schwarzenegger. Arnold would probably still dominate me in a pose off in his 60s, but never in a race to the puck. For hockey specific performance, getting 15-20% of calories from protein is ideal. Also remember sufficient carbs (55-75% of calories) must be consumed to provide the body with enough energy for the protein to be useful.

TIPS:

- 1 oz. of any protein from the below spreadsheet is equal to any one of the items in that category. In other words 1oz. of beef = 1 oz. of fish = 1 oz. of chicken, etc. from within the very lean meat category.
- Fresh is better than frozen.
- With poultry, take the skin off to reduce fat calories. Also, white meat (breasts, wings) is less fatty than dark meat (thighs).
- Some items such as chipped beef, Canadian bacon, American cheddar cheese, and processed hot dogs tend to have 400 mg or more of sodium per 1oz exchange. These foods will dehydrate you.
- Veal, lamb and beef are all considered red meat. The up side of red meat is it contains iron, zinc, and B vitamins which help carry oxygen to muscles, keeps your immunity strong, and aids in healing/recovery times. (All important aspects of peak performance). The down side of red meat is the type of fat contained in it isn't so healthy.
- Bottom line: choose leaner cuts and keep portions reasonable. 'Cut' refers to where on the animal's body the meat comes from. Loin and round are the leanest cuts. **The USDA lists 7 cuts of beef that meet their guidelines for lean: eye round, top round, round tip, top sirloin, and bottom round, to loin, tenderloin, and flank steak**.
- Grade' is used to further determine the kind of meat. 'Prime' has the most fat, 'choice' has second highest, 'select' is leaner still. The cut and grade should appear on the label in the grocery store. (If the only form of cooking you know how to do involves a BBQ then reread the above section. You can impress your friends, ladies, and neighborhood butcher while improving your hockey performance.)

Very Lean Meat ***(1oz)*** ***(7 g protein, 0-1 g fat, 35 cal)***	**Lean Meat (1oz)** ***(7 g protein, 3 g fat, 55 cal)***	**Medium Fat Meat** ***(1oz)*** ***(7 g protein, 5 g fat, 75 cal)***	**High Fat Meat** ***(1oz)*** ***(7g protein, 8 g fat, 100 cal)***
Beans, peas, lentils (cooked) 1/2cup	**Cheese:** 4.5% fat cottage (1/4 cup), grated parmesan 2 tbsp, cheeses with 3 g or less fat per oz	**Egg** (limit 8 per week), soy milk, tofu	**Cheese:** all regular cheese
Fish: cod, haddock, flounder, halibut, tuna, tuna canned in water, trout	**Fish:** herring (uncreamed or smoked), oysters, salmon 9fresh/canned), catfish, sardines (canned), tuna (canned in oil, drained)	**Cheese** with 5 g or less fat per oz, feta, mozzarella, ricotta ¼	**Pork:** spareribs, ground pork, pork sausage
Poultry: chicken, turkey, cornish hen, duck, pheasant	**Poultry:** chicken, turkey (dark meat, no skin), chicken (white meat, with skin), domestic duck or goose (well-drained of	**Fish:** any fried fish product	Processed sandwich meat with 8 g or less fat per oz, bologna, pimento loaf, salami, sausage, bratwurst, Italian knockwurst, polish smoked, hot dog, bacon

Game: venison, buffalo, antelope, ostrich	Goose (no skin), rabbit Veal: lean chop, roast	**Poultry:** chicken (dark meat, with skin), ground turkey or ground chicken, friend chicken (with skin)fat no skin)	
Cheese with 1 g or less fat per oz: -Nonfat or law-fat cottage cheese ¼ c. -fat-free cheese 1 oz	**Beef:** USDA select or choice grades of lean beef trimmed of ft, such as round, sirloin, and flank steak; tenderloin; roast (rib, chuck, rump); steak 9t-bone, porterhouse, cubed) ground round Lamb: roast, chop, leg	**Veal**: cutlet (ground or cubed, unbreaded)	
Other: **Egg whites** 2 Kidney (high cholesterol) 1 oz Sausage with 1 g or less fat per oz 1 oz Hot dogs with	**Pork**: lean pork, such as fresh ham; canned, cured, or boiled ham; Canadian bacon; tenderloin, center loin chop	**Beef:** most beef products fall into this category (ground beef, meatloaf, corned beef, short ribs, prime grades, or meat	

1 g or less fat per oz 1oz Processed sandwich meat with 1 g or less fat per oz: deli thin sliced, shaved meats, chipped beef, turkey ham 1oz		trimmed of fat. Lamb rib roast, ground	
	Hot dogs with 3 g or less fat per oz, processed sandwich meat with 3 g or less fat pre oz, such as turkey, pastrami, or kielbasa, liver, heart	**Pork:** top loin, chop, Boston butt, cutlet	

- Processed meats, such as hot dogs, sausage, bologna, and salami are all usually high in fat.

Game Day Hot Tip: Have a carb/protein shake drink ready to drink immediately (0-10 minutes) after the game… it might be worth bringing along your own blender!

Key #4 FATS

When it comes to fat, the key is very simple … good fats are good for you and bad fats are bad for you. It's not rocket science. Good fats are critical to cellular repair, regulating blood sugar, aiding in your mental ability, and memory retention. Make sure to read the labels. You want mono or polyunsaturated which are good, while saturated fats should only be taken in moderate consumption. Avoid trans-fats all together. *(Most fast food restaurants have completely stopped using foods and cooking oils containing trans-fat which should give you a good idea how bad they're for you).* Use oils in dark glass containers (olive, sunflower or safflower oils) including Omega 6 and omega 3 fatty acids in 3:1 ratio which is critical.

Essential fatty acids are just that, essential to your body functioning properly. Our bodies aren't capable of manufacturing them, so we must consume the right amount to be properly balanced. The challenge for most people isn't the quantity of fat they consume, but rather making healthy choices. Eat unsaturated sources to obtain the desired amount of fat (refer to chart). For the most part, just recognize which foods are known to contain which fats. **If you eat a lot of food in the bad fat and trans-fat column you will feel sluggish and mentally unmotivated.** *(Just think back to the last time you crushed a Big Mac or Whopper combo. You didn't exactly feel energized after the fact did you?)* When you go to the grocery store or cook for your self, use the good fat options when it's called for and you will notice the difference.

Good Fat Mono or polyunsaturated = good	**Bad Fat Saturated = moderate consumption**	**Trans Fat Avoid**
Nuts and seeds		Partially hydrogenated
Nut Butter	High fat meats	Cookies
Fish (high fat)	Butter	Crackers
Fish Oil (supplement)	Cream	Pie
Olive Oil/ Canola	High fat dairy	Processed food
Flaxseed Oil	Mayonnaise	
Ground Flax	Most salad dressing	
*store oils in dark glass containers		

TIPS:

- Remember healthy options if and when:
  ----you have a lot of favorite foods in the non-beneficial category. What to do …
  1. Decrease the frequency of eating them
  2. Decrease the portion size
  3. Substitute healthy options in their place (e.g. use mustard or salsa instead of mayo)
  4. Eliminate that choice all together
  5. **Don't be afraid of eating them, but do it in moderation and definitely don't over do it!**
- Consider adding a fish oil supplement into your daily routine.
- 20-30% of your total calories may come from good fats.
- If calorie needs are very high, consider increasing fat to 40% from heart healthy sources like nuts, nut butters,

olive oil or avocado. Guacamole made from avocado is a great dip instead of ranch or any other cream based sauce. *(Ranch is my favorite dip so I feel your pain.)*

- Extra Virgin Olive Oil and cold pressed organic canola oil are preferable oils to use in salad and cooking because of their inherent properties.

Game Day Hot Tip: We all recognize that sometimes something sweet like chocolate, cookies, or ice cream hits the spot. Indulge occasionally, but be sure to branch out and more times than not use healthy choices. A lot of these options provide unhealthy fats. Be aware of the fatty meats that pack a lot of sodium. Eat it on an off day or as a treat after a post game meal.

Key #5 YOUR DAILY NUTRITION SCHEDULE

"Over the course of my McDiet, I consumed 30 pounds of sugar from their food. That's a pound a day. On top of that, I also took in 12 pounds of fat. Now, I know what you're saying. You're saying nobody's supposed to eat this food three times a day. No wonder all this stuff happened to you. But the scary part is: there are people who eat this food regularly. Some people even eat it every day."

----Supersize Me (2004)

As an elite athlete you want to stay energized and alert. You don't want to experience energy roller coasters during the day. More and more of the research is suggesting 5-6 smaller meals throughout the day. A regular eating pattern helps to control appetite, regulate blood sugar (so as not to overwork the pancreas), reduces the blood sugar spikes and dips, eliminates mood swings and reduces over eating which will foster leaner body mass. If you are an athlete trying to gain muscle mass, smaller more regular meals makes getting the necessary amount of calories easier than trying to stuff your face until you pop in less meals. (It was always funny to watch the big lineman where I went to school at Notre Dame eat. They must have had 3,000 calories every meal and snack bags in between.) The 5-6 meal approach gives you a smoother and more efficient energy ride.

TIPS:

- In order to maintain a consistent, healthy eating schedule you need to plan well. Surround yourself with quality food and always have it accessible. This means ***PLANNING!***
- Prepare meals in advance and use bulk cooking methods. (When barbecuing or making pasta, make enough for 3 meals and store the rest in the refrigerator. It gives you two quick easy meals or snacks for the next couple of days.)
- Have a well stocked refrigerator.
- Travel with water, food and healthy snacks in your backpack, car, airplane travel bag, etc. (I found Solo Bars to be the best tasting energy bars on the market. Lots of flavors, easy to pack and they provide that lasting energy.)
- Fight the temptation for fast food by using proper planning and discipline.
- Eating something is always better than nothing. Make any food coming into your mouth a mini-meal. What you put into your body is just as in important—maybe even more--as how you train and practice. **THINK LIKE A PRO ATHLETE**. How will each bite of food affect your energy levels and overall performance?
- Consider adding a multivitamin with an anti-oxidant complex into your daily routine.

Game Day Hot Tip: Maintaining optimal health by getting nutrients from whole foods in a varied diet is preferable to taking supplements as a substitute.

Key #6 "BREAK" THE FAST

Eat breakfast everyday. This is your most important meal of the day. Eating almost anything is better than nothing because your body has fasted all night. While you were sleeping and dreaming of scoring goals, girls, or both; your body was trying to rejuvenate its energy levels. Every college student at my school had to swipe our IDs at the dining hall. Little did we know at first that our trainer got a printout of everyone on the team's eating schedule. And as I said before, when you stay up late studying or dominating your roommate in Xbox and miss breakfast then there was hell to pay in the weight room. It's that important that the trainer will get in your face *(happened)* to get you to eat breakfast. Protein, carbs, and vegetables are a must. If there's any doubt, start with a shake. Breakfast provides energy, fuels the brain, and increases metabolism. Start your day off right, break the fast! Good breakfast choices would be eggs, oatmeal, whole grain cereal, yogurt, whole wheat toast, peanut butter (natural/organic), any fruit, muesli, whole wheat pancakes or wheat waffles.

TIP:

- As soon as you wake up drink 8oz of water. Hot lemon water relaxes the digestive system and energizes blood circulation.
- Crack an egg in the middle and pour the yoke from one half shell to the other over a bowl. Easy way to separate the egg white which drips into the bowl.

Game Day Hot Tip: *Do Not* skip breakfast on a game day and stay away from donuts and other sugary/dough options. If you're lucky enough to have a pre-game skate in the morning then divide your morning meal in half. Eat half the calories when you get up and eat the other half after the skate. For example on the road you usually have a choice of eggs, toast, cereal, bacon, hash browns, French toast and ham. Instead of crushing a couple of bowls of cereal, a dish of powdered eggs, French toast, and bacon—simple eat half of what you normally would. This will let you get the most out of the pre-game skate. Then have a hearty snack and make sure to hydrate after practice. This will replenish anything lost during the sweat.

Key #7 LUNCH AND DINNER

Optimal performance nutrition seeks to balance the diet for maximum energy, lean muscle mass, and regulation of blood sugar. Wholesome carbohydrates, lean meats, and vegetables need to be consumed in combination together. Take time to eat. Reread this chapter as many times as needed to get a full understanding of the right foods to eat for game time energy. Learn how to cook a few quick healthy meals even if you have to force yourself. This will save you money and time. Another important aspect is actually sitting down and enjoying the meals so it becomes a routine. Forget about the T.V., internet, texting, or whatever else you waste time doing. It only takes 5-10 minutes to eat and concentrate. Good choices for lunch/dinner would be: lean meat, whole grain bread, whole wheat pasta or couscous, brown rice, oats, barley, wild rice, bulgar, and buckwheat.

Game Day Hot Tip: Trial and error is your best friend. Take notes in a journal or log book. Keep track of foods you may react uncomfortably too (i.e., heart burn, more gaseous, after taste, constipation) or if certain meals leave you feeling lethargic instead of energized. I can't stress this enough. Many people react differently to the same meal. For optimal performance these days, some athletes go so far as to measure the minute mineral levels in their blood. That seems a little over the top to me, but something as simple as writing down the exact foods you ate and then monitoring your energy level with a 1-5 scale, quickly provides a basis for meals going forward. You will soon be an expert at determining what meals are best for you on game day.

Key #8 FRUITS AND VEGETABLES

Plants use sunlight to make starches, our primary source of complex carbohydrates. They are full of oils, vitamins, and minerals. Most fruit and vegetables are naturally high in fiber and low in cholesterol, rich in polyunsaturates, and essential amino acids and fatty acids. They don't contain any harmful saturated fats or trans-fatty acids. Fruits and vegetables are a big part of an energy rich diet and primarily where we get our vitamin C and vitamin A. Vitamin C facilitates the healing process. Bell peppers, papaya, cantaloupe and oranges are good sources of vitamin C. Vitamin A helps make white blood cells for fighting infection and repairing micro tears. Carrots, sweet potatoes, dried apricots, and spinach is good sources of vitamin A. Most people neglect this part of their diet. I know I do. Find a couple of fruits and vegetables that you like and mix them into your sides throughout the 6 meals. If you include a few of the above options in your daily meals along with taking a simple vitamin supplement, then you won't have to worry about getting your daily dose of vitamins.

TIPS:

- Eat fresh, organic food whenever possible. (You want to avoid the herbicides, pesticides or other agrochemicals found in conventionally farmed foods).
- Eat them raw whenever possible.
- Fresh vegetables should be firm and colorful. The deeper the color of the fruits and vegetables, the higher the antioxidant activity and nutritional energy value.
- Proper cleaning is essential. When removing skins, peel as finely as possible to preserve vital nutrients.
- Avoid soaking.
- Bananas should be fully ripe; peaches weighty; oranges and grapefruits smooth; grapes with green stems; sweet smelling melons and pineapple; and avoid strawberries

with white tips.

- When cooking, steam but make sure to keep the vegetables crunchy.
- If you need extra calories, sauté – do not fry.
- Fresh is best, frozen is second best, both are better than canned or processed as far as nutritional value is concerned.

Game Day Hot Tip: Fruits and veggies are your friend. Stick to fresh whenever possible. Always have a piece or two in your snack bag. Dried fruits are great high caloric choices when you need a pick me up, but be sure to drink a bit of extra water for re-hydrating with it.

Key #9 POST EXERCISE

After exercising, whether from a workout or competition, the body is dehydrated, blood insulin is low, muscle and liver glycogen is reduced or depleted, your muscles are in catabolic state with increased proteolysis, your immune system is suppressed, and cortisol as well as other catabolic hormones are elevated, (Athletes Performance Nutrition, John Ivy). To convert this post exercise state of your body to an anabolic state requires awareness of what, how, and most importantly when you should restore your body with the correct foods. Fortunately, much research has uncovered critical time windows for nutrient delivery to the muscles and cells. But most importantly within the first 10 minutes of finishing your exercise, a carbohydrate and protein supplement—shake or smoothie-- is recommended with a 2:1 or 3:1 carb to protein ratio. This will:

- Re-hydrate your body
- Increase blood insulin levels.
- Increase the rate of muscle glycogen.

- Increase the rate of muscle protein synthesis.
- Limit the suppression of the immune system
- Reduce muscle damage and speed its repair.
- Increase performance in future exercises. **(This is critical to remember.)**

When possible, within one hour make sure to have your post-game or post-workout meal.

Game Day Hot Tip: This is one of the biggest factors in determining your ability to rejuvenate for the next game. This is especially true with the football-like physical nature of hockey and also the marathon-like season of basketball. (The strength and conditioning it takes to sustain your self over a complete season has always amazed me.) Get the most out of your on-ice performance with great pre-game nutrition and sustain that same level of play over future games by supplying your body with a great post workout meal. And don't forget hydration. This requires planning ahead and being prepared.

Key #10 GROCERY LIST

A good shopper will stick to the outside of the grocery store and ignore the middle aisles as much as possible. The middle aisles tend to be full of highly processed food with no fiber. Most of these foods also contain partially hydrogenated oils which should be avoided. Remember the more natural (less processed) your choice, the better. Stock your house, car, gym bag, locker, office, etc. with healthy choices so proper nutrition is always within reach. To save money and avoid impulse buying, sit down and make a list of what you need for the week's workouts, games, and practices. Make sure you have a good understanding of the right foods. If not, you will be analyzing the nutritional sidebar on the box of every food you purchase.

TIPS:

Carbohydrates/grains/beans

- Look for whole wheat – bread, pasta, and couscous.
- Look for dark bread – pumpernickel, bran, sour dough
- Look for beans – black, kidney, pinto, navy
- Look for brown rice

Fruits/Vegetables

- All fruits and vegetables are good. Fresh is best, frozen is second best. Avoid canned.
- Use all the colors of the rainbow. Generally, the more color the more nutritional value.
- Pre-cut and package your food so it's ready to go whenever needed. Have an endless supply of Ziploc bags (sandwich and gallon size) and plastic cartons so you can package and store any leftovers.

Nuts/Seeds/ Healthy Fats

- Make your own dressing with balsamic or red wine vinegar. It doesn't take a long time or require much skill plus they're low calorie and great tasting.
- Choose low fat salad dressing. *(I feel you. I'm a huge fan of blue cheese so this one hurts. But even fatty choices like Blue Cheese or Ranch have low-fat options that taste pretty good.)*
- Use olive, canola, and safflower oils.
- Good choices of nuts include: almonds, walnuts, pecans, and sunflower seeds (watch the sodium in these though). A cutting edge diet from Russia advocates eating a lot of almonds for their energy value. Just something to consider.
- Avocado – make your own guacamole. *(It's very simple and as a bonus you can whip this up at any party in less than 5 minutes. Then you're always a high draft pick come Super Bowl time.)*
- Natural peanut butter. There should be a noticeable amount of oil in the jar. Just stir it.

Meats/Proteins - *see spreadsheet chart on protein

Dairy

- Low fat milk, cheese, cottage cheese, yogurt and ice cream. (Be careful with dairy as this can mess with your stomach and pack on the lbs.)

Non-Dairy (Take this as it is. If you feel like too much of a vegan, then one-time a steak after Saturday night's game)

- Almond milk
- Plain organic soy yogurt
- Soy milk
- Rice milk

Vitamins

- Consider supplementation for :
  a) Fish oil/essential fatty acids
  b) Multi-vitamin
  c) Anti-oxidant complex
  d) Calcium

(Do your homework before you start downing supplements or pills. At best it provides a slight boost to your game, and at worst it becomes very expensive urine.)

Sweeteners (Lots of sugar in some of these options so be careful)

- Maple syrup (some brands are terrible. Be conscious of what you're buying)
- Honey

Game Day Hot Tip: Nutritionally your biggest downfall is not preparing and then being forced to opt for the fast food choice. I know we all have a buddy that puts on his equipment while eating a Big Mac meal, then skates rings around the other team. The thing is, what if he/she was disciplined enough to eat right. Instead of 50 goals a season, he might have 65. You never know. Make the most out of the talent you have by preparing as best you know how. Get disciplined with your grocery shopping and take a few minutes to prep your own veggie sticks (carrots and celery are tried and true choices), trail mix, or an energy bar/shake and you won't be caught without a healthy choice.

Key #11 TRAVELING STRATEGIES

Do's

- Do take control of your food choices (make decisions with your head, not your stomach or eyes)
- Do stay hydrated (especially with air travel)
- Do eat every 3 hours (6 meals a day)
- Do bring bars and shakes for snacks and pre/post workout nutrition
- Do have a lean protein choice with each meal

Don'ts

- Don't let your stomach get the best of you
- Don't skip meals
- Don't eat anything fried
- Don't travel without some of the following: nuts and seeds, beef jerky, fig newtons, fresh fruit, granola bars, meal replacement bars, green tea bags, and bottled water.

Eating Out – In General

The best option is to plan ahead and bring your own food. If you must eat out, remember you're fueling for peak performance. Typically, fast food establishments are not the best choices. However with some discipline and specific requests you can make the best of it. Keep in mind:

- Choose water. (Any form of carbonation is said to break down the muscle building process. Most soda is full of sugar.)
- NO FRIED food.

- Choose a baked potato or salad as a side.
- GO GRILLED!!!
- Choose proteins with the least amount of legs first …(i.e., fish, then chicken, then beef)
- TAKE OFF THE SKIN. Chicken or turkey – remove the skin.
- Hold on the sauces, especially mayonnaise

Eating out:

- Look for grilled fish or chicken
- If you choose steak, make it a cut that's less marbled and then trim the fat yourself.
- Save salad with low fat dressing or vinaigrette for the end.
- Have steamed vegetables, not fries.
- Use moderation with potato dishes and bread rolls – lay off butter or margarine, sour cream, bacon bits and other add-ons.

Airports:

- At food courts look for sandwich shops and bring something onto the plane. Keep snacks and water accessible for the flight. (New restrictions are pretty restrictive when is comes to water. The good news is that on the plane the flight attendants are more liberal with the H2O. Keep it coming.)

Gas stations:

- Grab water, dried fruits and nuts, beef jerky, energy bars, granola bars, and low calorie tea drinks.

I realize the hockey season is a bunch of road games that you need to travel to by car, plane, or bus. As much as I hope that you come prepared and pack for every possible option, I know that's not always realistic. The team bus or a teammate's parent giving you a lift might have the GPS set for the local fast food joint. As you can tell by North America's expanding waistline, this isn't always the right option. However you can minimize the negative effects by understanding what to eat and knowing a few healthy options from some of the most popular fast food restaurants. If I left any of your favorite restaurants off the list I apologize. After developing a nasty habit of dominating burgers at the West Coast burger chain called IN/OUT, I can understand the intense commitment to your favorite fast food restaurants. Tim Horton's still has a place in my heart. But enough with the fond memories, let's figure out the right foods to eat in a crunch at the most popular fast food restaurants.

Pizza (Pizza Hut/Papa John's/Domino's/etc)

- Go with thin crust veggie
- Then thin crust cheese or Hawaiian
- Add Grilled chicken to a salad or pizza
- Grab a salad with low-fat dressing
- No bread sticks.
- Stay away from extra cheese

McDonald's

- Chicken McGrill sandwich with BBQ sauce and a side salad with low-fat vinaigrette dressing
- Grilled Chicken Caesar (1/2 packet low-fat balsamic vinaigrette)
- Grilled Chicken California Cobb Salad (1/2 packet low-fat balsamic vinaigrette)
- Egg McMuffin or 2 scrambled Eggs with an English Muffin.
- Fruit and yogurt parfait

Wendy's

- Grilled Chicken Sandwich/side salad/ low fat dressing
- Garden Sensation Salads with low fat dressing
- Large chili /side salad/low fat dressing
- Small chili or baked potato with steamed broccoli

Arby's

- Grilled Chicken Deluxe/no mayo/ side salad/ low fat dressing
- Roast Beef/side salad/low fat dressing
- Turkey Club Salad/no bacon/low fat dressing
- Grilled chicken salad/low fat dressing
- Breakfast – sourdough with ham and egg

Boston Market

- Marinated Grilled Chicken with a side steamed vegetable medley and fresh fruit
- Rotisserie Turkey with green beans and fresh fruit
- Rotisserie chicken(no skin) with garlic potatoes and fresh fruit
- Oriental Grilled Chicken salad with ½ the dressing and no noodles
- Chicken Carver/no sauce and fresh fruit

Subway

- For bread options choose whole wheat or honey wheat
- Load up on the vegetables
- Make lean meat choices like turkey, roast beef and ham (tuna has a lot of mayo)
- If you're starving then choose extra meat instead of a side of chips. *(I've noticed that those sandwich artists respect the extra meat choice and will pack it high.)*

Taco Bell

- Say no to sour cream (It comes out of a sour cream gun. Enough said) hard taco shells that are fried, and go easy on cheese and guacamole.
- Chicken soft taco
- Bean burrito
- Chicken burrito
- Fiesta chicken burrito
- Taco salad and salsa
- *********Ordering fresco style decreases calorie and fat by about 25%*******

Baja Fresh

- Again say no to sour cream, and go easy on cheese and guacamole.
- Baja ensalada with salsa verde dressing
- Bare burrito with half the rice
- Mahi mahi ensalada
- 'side by side'
- Bean and cheese burrito
- 2 chicken taco chilitos

GAME DAY HOT TIP: Make decisions with your head, not with your stomach. For meals and snacks bring some of your own supplies to ensure you have high energy food. If for whatever reason you do stop at a fast food joint, pick your meal carefully. Don't let what your teammates or family eat effect what you order. How many games do you get the opportunity to play in a season? Don't ruin it because you have a craving for a greasy hamburger.

Key #12 HOW TO COOK

How you prepare your food is as important as the food you prepare. Breading a healthy chicken breast and frying it in trans-fat will ruin any nutritional value. Deep-frying ads saturated fat and empty calories you don't need. Be sure to use the healthy cooking methods below to get the most out of the foods you eat. If you don't cook, at least recognize the many methods of preparing meals. Here are some healthy tips to make the most out of your grocery list.

Steaming unlocks flavor and nutrients. Use a bamboo basket or collapsible steaming basket inside a saucepan with a ½ inch of water to steam your food. This is one of the best ways to flavor food while keeping nutrients intact. Vegetables should still be crunchy not soggy.

Broiling in the oven under a hot flame is a quick way to 'grill' your food. Broiling gives a great taste to meat, poultry, fish, and vegetables. Be careful when broiling food because if you're an amateur chef like me you can easily burn "anything" including your fingers or forearms. *(Someone needs to invent a full-arm oven mitt/sleeve for people like me.)*

Baking and roasting is used for cooking vegetables, potatoes, casseroles or meats in the oven. It's an easy and flavorful way to prepare a main or side dish.

Grilling over a hot flame or BBQing is a good way to prepare meat because it drains away excess fat. Just know which meats to cook. I prepare 98% percent of my meals this way. It's easy to do and absolutely essential to learn for life after 20. You can marinate meat, fish, and vegetables before cooking to add flavor.

Slow cooking is simmering at a low temperature over an extended period of time. If you've ever seen the famous scene in the gangster movie *Goodfellas* where Ray Liotta's character lectures on the importance of stewing pasta sauce over a long time period, then you understand this concept. Preparing food this way retains the nutrients and creates tender stews and beans. The food will remain moist because the pot is covered. Most of you won't or don't have the time to use this cooking option, however your billet mom will definitely put this on the table, so now you can nod and eat her food in peace.

Poaching gently simmers the food with liquid. Use a fish poacher or saucepan for keeping cooked fish moist and flavorful. Using a saucepan of gently boiling water to poach an egg cooks it without the use of oil.

Low-moisture cooking seals in the natural flavors and nutrients, while preserving color and texture. Brown your meats without oil, then add a little liquid and cover to cook. Place vegetables in a small amount of water, cover and steam until tender.

<u>Sauté or stir-fry</u> small pieces of vegetables or thin slices of meat in a sauté pan or non-stick frying pan with a small amount of olive oil for a quick way to prepare a healthy meal in minutes.

Quick Guide to establish serving sizes:

- 1 hand size = 6 oz serving of fish, poultry or red meat
- 2 thumbnails = 1 oz of hard cheeses
- 1 thumb = 1 tablespoon of olive, flax or plant oils
- 1 handful = 1 oz of nuts and seeds
- 1 fist size = 1 cup whole grains, legumes, yogurt

GAME DAY HOT TIP: Make sure your meals contain as many servings of fruit and vegetables as you can handle. Leaving the skin on vegetables helps retain nutrients and moisture.

---

*AVOID MICROWAVING AS MUCH AS POSSIBLE. DON'T EVEN RE-HEAT FOOD IN IT!!!

Key # 13 Sleep

Sleep is the most important non-nutrient you can incorporate into your daily habits. While we sleep we carry on functions of cleansing and rebuilding that we can not get even from resting. For instance, our liver cleanses during sleep. Good sleep revitalizes tired bodies, gives you more energy, and helps you think more clearly during the day. Given the game day schedule for hockey players (game ends at 10:30 pm then a post game bike ride, meal, add on the drive home plus the time it takes for the body to calm down and it's already at least 2 am) makes the mid-day nap critical to getting the necessary amount of sleep.

Here are some pointers from "the man" Tim Ferris on his blog into what he has found to help him:

Here are a few effective techniques and hacks I've picked up over the last five years from sources ranging from biochemistry PhDs to biologists at Stanford University…

1. Consume 150-250 calories of low-glycemic index foods in small quantities (low glycemic load) prior to bed.

Morning fatigue and headache isn't just from sleep debt or poor sleep. Low blood sugar following overnight fasting is often a contributing factor. Just prior to bed, have a small snack such as: a few sticks of celery with almond butter, a mandarin orange and 5-8 almonds, or plain low-fat (not fat-free) yogurt and an apple. Ever wonder how you can sleep 8-10 hours and feel tired? This is part of the explanation. Make a pre-bed snack part of your nutritional program.

1-2 tablespoons of flaxseed oil (120-240 calories) can be used in combination with the above to further increase cell repair during sleep and thus decrease fatigue. It tastes like a mixture of cat urine and asparagus, so I recommend pinching your nose while consuming it — thanks Seth Roberts, PhD. for this tip — or using capsules.

2. Turn off preoccupation with afternoon closure and present-state training.

I have — as do most males in my family — what is called "onset insomnia." I don't have trouble staying asleep, but I have a difficult time falling asleep, sometime laying awake in bed for 1-2 hours. There are two approaches that I've used with good effect without medications to address this: 1) Determine and set a top priorities to-do list that afternoon for the following day to avoid late-night planning, 2) Do not read non-fiction prior to bed, which encourages projection into the future and preoccupation/planning. Read fiction that engages the imagination and demands present-state attention.

Getting a goodnight sleep accomplishes everything from fat-loss (leptin release decreases with sleep debt) to memory consolidation, sleep is the currency of high-performance living.[15]

[15] http://www.fourhourworkweek.com/blog/2008/01/27/relax-like-a-pro-5-steps-to-hacking-your-sleep/

Summary of the Nutrition Chapter

- The hockey season is a marathon consisting of 82 sprints. In order to optimize your energy and performance you need to develop great everyday nutritional habits as well as put the right foods into your body before game time.

- The best long term investment you can make for your body to be fit and function at peak performance levels is to eat and especially drink in a healthy manner.

There are **13 Keys** highlighted in the book:

1. **Hydration**
   a. Even minor dehydration impairs contractile strength in the muscles, speed, concentration, coordination, reaction time, and stamina.
   b. As a guideline try to drink 1/2oz -1oz per pound/per day.
2. **Carbohydrates**
   a. These are found only in products made from plants.
   b. Athletes should strive to get 55-65% of their calories from carbs (20-25 cal per pound).
   c. The best foods to choose are the ones least processed.
   d. Know the glycemic index and digestion times of game day foods.
3. **Proteins**
   a. Proteins are the building blocks of the body.
   b. Not all proteins are created equal. Choose leaner cuts and keep portions under control.
   c. For hockey specific performance getting 15-20% of calories from protein is ideal.
4. **Fats**
   a. This is very simple ... good fats are good for you

and bad fats are bad for you. Mono or polyunsaturated are good. Saturated fats should be moderately consumed. Trans fats are terrible and needless to say should not be eaten.

b. Look at the fat column. Recognize which foods are known to contain which fats.

c. Substitute healthy options in their place (e.g. use mustard or salsa instead of mayo)

5. **Daily Eating Habits**

   a. 5-6 smaller portioned meals throughout the day will keep you alert and energized. You won't experience energy spikes and dips.

   b. In order to maintain a consistent healthy eating schedule you need to plan well. Surround yourself with quality food and always have it accessible.

   c. Prepare meals in advance and use bulk preparation.

   d. Eating something is always better than nothing.

6. **Break the Fast**

   a. Eat breakfast everyday. This is your most important meal of the day.

   b. Breakfast provides energy, fuels the brain, and increases metabolism after not eating anything for 8-10 hours.

7. **Lunch and Dinner**

   a. This meal provides your game time energy. Very important

   b. Wholesome carbohydrates, lean meats, and vegetables need to be consumed in combination together.

   c. Learn how to cook a few quick healthy meals even if you have to force yourself.

   d. Take notes in a journal of any foods that you may react uncomfortable to, make you feel lethargic, or on the other hand provide you with the most energy. Everyone is different.

8. **Fruits and Vegetables**
    a. Fruits and vegetables are a big part of an energy rich diet and primarily where we get our vitamin A and vitamin C.
    b. Eat raw organic fruits and vegetables whenever possible.
    c. Fresh is best, frozen is second best, both are better than canned or processed as far as nutritional value is concerned.
9. **Post Exercise**
    a. Have a shake or smoothie ready to consume within 10-15 minutes after a workout or game.
    b. When possible, within 45 minutes make sure to have your post-game or post-workout meal.
    c. Know the correct foods needed to replenish lost energy stores.
    d. Remember to hydrate.
10. **Grocery List**
    a. Make sure you have a good understanding of the right foods.
    b. Get disciplined with your grocery shopping
    c. Stay away from pre-made meals
11. **Traveling Strategies**
    a. Make sure to stay hydrated and bring snacks to munch on.
    a. The best option is to plan ahead and bring your own food.
    b. Quick Substitutes
        i. Choose grilled over fried
        ii. Choose mustard over mayonnaise
        iii. Choose salad over french fries
        iv. Choose water over soda
        v. Choose chicken over a burger
        vi. Choose wheat over white bread

12. **How to Cook**
    a. How you prepare your food is as important as the food you prepare
    b. Use healthy cooking methods to get the most out of the foods you eat.
13. **Sleep**
    a. While we sleep we carry on functions of cleansing and rebuilding.
    b. Consume 150-250 calories of **low-glycemic index** foods in small quantities (low **glycemic load**) prior to bed.

Routines

Routines

Reggie Dunlop: What are you guys doing?
Steve Hanson: Putting on the foil!
Jeff Hanson: Every game!
Jack Hanson: Yeah, you want some?
---Slapshot (1977)

Pick up the remote and turn the channel to any sporting event. You're going to see countless routines performed by the players. They happen all the time right under you nose, but you've just never realized it. For instance, a baseball player makes the sign of the cross then digs into the batter's box the exact same way every time he gets up. A basketball player tugs at his uniform then bounces the ball 3 times before he shoots a free throw. A 100 meter sprinter jumps two times then gets set in the blocks. Football linemen with arms the size of my waist, slap each other before every game. It's not just for show. These are all pre-game routines performed before the opening play and a lot of times during the game.

A routine usually starts when a player copies something they saw or did and then they have a successful game or individual play. Then the player associated that specific thing to his success and repeated it the next game. Take a goalie for instance. They may tap both posts before a game and get a shutout. The next game he remembers that and taps both posts again. After a few successful times it becomes a routine. A pro knows it's not the specific action that caused the success, but rather the state of mind the routine attracts. When the goalie taps both posts, it brings back positive memories about his prior shutout. This will build his confidence at the crucial time needed before a game. According to the book *Mind Gym* by Gary Mack and David Casstevens "the conscious practice of routines leads to the unconscious habit of success. Routines are comforting mechanisms---triggering mechanisms. Every athlete has his own routine, whether consciously or unconsciously that puts them in game state."[16]

A lot of the above scenarios are performed in the spur of the moment. This will definitely help the athlete in the present, but this section focuses on the entire day's activities leading up to the game. These routines eliminate distractions, narrow focus for the tasks ahead; keep a player emotionally stable no matter how important the game, and also help the player "shut off" his brain to the negative thoughts/doubts he may have concerning the upcoming game.

Hockey players, more than other athletes in different sports are known to have a number of "idiosyncrasies." This may be due to the 80 game schedules or the physical nature of the game, which both require tremendous focus every time you step on the ice. During my playing days I noticed that different players used different routines to get prepared. Certain players rely more heavily on routines. Take goaltenders for instance. Even their wives know to leave them alone on game days. And then you have some players battling it out in video games right up until they leave to the rink. No matter where you lay on the spectrum, the importance is that routines affect your performance. The goal of this chapter is to make you aware of your current routine and highlight some changes to improve your on-ice performance. If you don't have a current routine then this chapter will provide a few examples and an outline to begin one. If you do have a routine then this chapter will show you how it affects your game and where you can make changes to improve it. First we'll start with an explanation of the routine and the mental aspect associated with it.

---

[16] *Mind Gym*, Gary Mack and David Casstevens, McGraw- Hill, 2001

Too much of a Good Thing is Bad

Is it possible to have too much of a good thing? In excess most things take on characteristics of their opposites. Thus:

- Your significant other or yourself complains about nothing to wear with a closet full of clothes
- Summer vacation is great at first but then becomes extremely boring
- You catch too many fish and you get tired, limit out, and have to go home
- Your house has a huge backyard. You have to mow it.
- You have one beer it's great. You have 10 it's bad times.

Too much, too many, and too often of anything that you wish for becomes annoying at first and then downright unbearable. It's like the old fable where anything you touch turns to gold. Consider the parental trick/punishment of feeding an entire pack of smokes to a teenager caught smoking. When dealing with routines in this chapter, it can easily be taken to an extreme that will negatively affect your game. The goal of this chapter isn't to turn you into an obsessive head case with a thousand routines that you stack upon each other to get mentally prepared. That would be defeating the purpose and even create more of the distractions you're trying to avoid. The goal of this chapter is to provide you with first, the knowledge of how routines are used to create focus. Then secondly, provide a number of routines that you can choose from to help you begin your own pre-game rituals. Be aware of taking this chapter and using it as a crutch for your game. All the advice in this chapter, book, and life should be taken with a grain of salt, critically examined by yourself, and then implemented if it helps you. **The**

following routines are meant to help you prepare for every game. Each routine will help your pre-game preparation which leads to a consistently better performance, night in and night out. The following list of routines for players could be endless and everyone is very different, but here's a small portion of what players at the pro level do before a game. ***Feel free to use any of the listed suggestions but by no means do you want to take the whole list and work it all into your pre-game routine. Then your routine would become complicated and stressful which is counterproductive to playing well. If you think you're game will suffer because you missed a step in your routine for whatever reason, then the routine has turned against you. It becomes a hooky superstition. Sometimes players feel superstitions need to be performed or else the sky will come crashing down, ruining their game. It becomes a mental block and completely dictates your game. It's not preparation but simple a quick fix to duct tape up a mental deficiency. This will not allow you to perform consistently at your top level. As soon as your game starts to suffer in this instance then you will need to switch up the superstition.*** **Your routine keeps you grounded in the present to further enhance your game. Do not make it the main focus of your day with the game coming in second. If you notice yourself becoming a little OCD then adjust your routine and also your thinking. The routine should become an effortless way to get ready for the game.**

What is a routine?

A routine is a specific action performed over and over again that produces predictable mental and physical results leading up to the game or individual play. These results can be good in that they get you into the right state of mind for optimal performance. Or they can also be debilitating by creating personal doubt, which generates timidity and overall negatively affects your game. Some parts of your current routine—which you probably don't consciously realize you're doing--may be severely affecting your game. We want to eliminate the bad and incorporate the good into your personal routine. As stated above, a good routine will eliminate distractions, keeps you in the present moment to stop any negative thoughts or doubts, psychologically prepares you for the game, and keeps your nerves and energy from spiking or dipping with the perceived importance of the game.

A good routine will ultimately eliminate distractions. Whether you're a squirt worried about the post game pizza party, a college player thinking about final exams, or a pro worried about the media, the game day routine will center all your thoughts and effort on the upcoming game. Sometimes everything going on besides the game can pile up which leads your mind to wander. This can become a huge problem on game day. Even announcers do their homework on major crises in a player's life. If they uncover any situation such as their wife having a baby or maybe the player was reportedly seen out late during a playoff series, then they question his game readiness on national TV. The greatest example I can think of occurred when Brett Favre's dad passed away. No one would have thought less of him if he didn't play under those circumstances. No one would have expected him to be prepared and play well. But he ran onto the field, mentally ready and played the best game of his entire life in a Monday night football game where he passed for 399 yards. The trick isn't to pretend that life's circumstances aren't weighing you down, but to push them out of your mind for the immediate game. Joe Paterno, the most famous college football coach of all time, divides the Penn State campus with an imaginary blue line separating school from the football complex. Papa Joe tells players that before they cross that imaginary blue line on the way to campus he expects them to dump all of their worries and concerns. Once the players' steps across the line, they cannot be thinking about there grades, girlfriends, or even have their cell phone on. The minute he crosses the line his mind should be focused on Penn State football and nothing else. If it isn't, he's shortchanging himself as an athlete. He is also hurting the team.

The minute you start your pre-game routine, your mind recognizes the familiarity and focuses on the next step in the routine, instead of the other thoughts or feelings racing around your head a million mph. **Your mind thinks I've done this before and I can do it again.** Nothing else matters but the next step followed by the next step followed by the next step in the routine until all of a sudden you burst out of the runway onto the ice. By simply completing one part of the routine and moving to the next part, you stay completely in the present. You don't give yourself a chance to think about the 2 million other things you need to do. This focus is crucial to the mental preparation needed for optimal performance.

"Each point I play is in the now moment. The last point means nothing, the next point means nothing."—Billie Jean King

As mentioned above a routine keeps the player completely in the present "now" moment. As you go through each step of the routine and concentrate on that specific activity your brain can't think of past thoughts like your 5-0 loss the last time you played this team or why you can't score against this particular goalie. These mind blocks are the exact opposite of helpful. The past has already happened. Hopefully you quickly learned the lesson from that mistake or mistakes and then completely forgot it every happened. Tonight's game is the only thing that counts and no doubt you will face similar experiences. **THIS TIME YOU WILL OWN IT.** The mind can only concentrate on one thing at a time. So, rather than suppress what you don't want to happen, you must focus on what you do want to happen. A set routine will help get you prepared. For example have you ever seen a pro meticulously tape each stick perfectly before a game? They're so into it that 10 minutes has gone by before they pick up their head.

If you could actually get inside their head, you might hear something like *"this is my game stick. It has great weight and just the right curve. The puck will be glued to this tape and I'm going to bury a few tonight. I've treated you right and now it's time to go."* Everything is positive and moving forward. There are no thoughts about past giveaways, missed nets, errant passes, or stickhandling mishaps. By taping your stick, individual stretching, running the stairs, or any number of the many steps you can incorporate into your routine, you're effectively staying in the present. There's no chance of going backward or forward on your hockey timeline so your mind can think up reasons to fail.

Routines done in the right manner also physically prepare you for the game. Without getting too technical, the mind groups certain routines with particular internal chemical responses. You will literally produce millions of chemicals stronger than any pharmaceutical drug with a quick glance from a member of the opposite sex or from scoring a goal. Everyday you go through daily habits that produce certain chemicals which affect your overall emotions. For instance most of us go through the same routine on weekdays. Wake up late after pounding the snooze button at least 3 times, shower, brush our teeth, and throw our wrinkled clothes on to go to school/work. As soon as your mind kicks into gear you immediately start thinking of the day's tasks. (The morning dose of caffeine is a way most adults affect their internal state upon waking) What do I need to do today, is my homework right or do I need to speak to my boss about this project? I'm not going to lie. Most of the everyday things we need to do sometimes become tedious. They create a nervous energy that you have to recognize and control or you will be in an anxious state all day. On the other hand when you wake up on a regular Saturday or Sunday you have a completely different routine (If you're not hung over. But then again we have routines for that scenario too.) You may sleep in, read the paper, grab some breakfast at the local bagel joint, and overall just chill out. This routine puts you in a completely different state. Everything moves in slow motion. The day is a little bit easier and a lot less stressful. If you could measure the body's internal chemical state, there would be a significant difference. And it all starts with the routine that you go through in the morning. Work or school is stressful but you put yourself in a stressful state before even getting to the office or classroom. Sunday's maybe relaxing or not, but you start the day off right and it usually stays positive throughout.

The same can be said of a game day routine leading up until the puck drops. As soon as you begin the first step in your game day routine, your mind recognizes this and internal changes begin to take place. As you move through the steps and get closer to the game, your body is amping up to play. If you develop a good routine with the necessary positive mindset, then this will occur without you thinking about it. You will be prepared. By the end of this chapter you will recognize—good and bad---the certain steps of your own routine. Then by using the outline provided, you will be able to add a number of different steps that work for you.

Have you ever heard the expression, some stages are just too big? Basically it's like telling someone that they can't handle the pressure and don't show up for important games. It's the worst knock you can get. But let's be realistic; some games are bigger than others. On these game days you actually feel a different atmosphere surrounding the rink. Everybody seems more tense, serious, and ready to snap at the smallest problem. The fans feel it, the trainers feel it, the coaches feel it, and you can't help but feel it. It can definitely be suffocating. If you let this surging tide drag you under, then you're done. You will either be so nervous and therefore prone to mistakes or so fired up that you take a stupid penalty. Not getting too high or too low emotionally is the trick. This allows you to think clearly and have complete control over your emotions. Many athletes refer to this place as the "zone". A routine will get you there.

The routine you adapt and use will be the same every game. No matter if it's a preseason inter-squad game or Game 7 of the Stanley Cup Finals. You are still going to go through the same steps in the same order. This will keep you in the present moment which stops you from thinking about the importance/lack of importance of tonight's game. If you begin to think about the weight of the game, your mind will increasingly escalate everything that "can" happen including negative scenarios. Mentally this is not where you want to be. You got to this point in the season by playing at a certain emotional level. This level is different for everyone but the optimal level for best performance doesn't individually change. Tonight's game may be the biggest game of your life but the routine will keep you grounded. Instead of your emotions and internal chemicals spiking or dipping depending on your thoughts, you will stay focused and maintain the right state. It also works the other way. If you are coming to the end of a tough road trip and you need to pull one out against a weak team before heading home, this will also work. Your mind drifts over a long season. Due to fatigue, injury, or a weak opponent your mind will play tricks on you and tell you in so many words to take it easy. Take the night off. That's when the routine kicks in. The routine will bring you back to the task at hand, which is playing your best and winning the game.

Your Current Routine and How to Develop a New One

"Amateur players have excellent games. Pro players have consistent game excellence."
-----Pat Riley

You have a routine that you go through prior to a game whether you know it or not. It could be as small as eating a Snickers bar before the game(not good) to Billy Smith-the New York Islanders goalie who won 4 Stanley Cups- who used to go into a solitude shell of concentration. He wouldn't talk to anyone including his wife. Many football players will check into a hotel room on Friday night because the transformation from nice guy to gridiron monster scares their family. Some steps in your routine help you prepare for the game and some hurt your preparation. We want to examine your current routine to eliminate the steps that may be causing you trouble on the ice and keep the ones working in your favor. We'll walk through each step in the process together. You may pay particular attention to one step over another or skip some of the steps altogether. The regular print will be an explanation of a particular step in the routine at a certain time leading up until the game. I ask you to think back to your last game and recall certain habits/rituals you did throughout the day. **The bold print will be things that pro players currently use that you might incorporate into your routine to help your game.**

Think back to your last game played. Realize that if most of your games are in the afternoon or morning then you will have a different routine then if you play at night, which is the timeline set out below.

7:30 pm The night before the game

First, let's start with your meal the night before the game. Did you think about what you ate and drank? All of us know it's probably not great to be funneling soda (beers for those of you old enough) and taking down 2 Big Macs. The proper hydration and nutrition is critical at this point. The routine starts with a great meal and proper fluids.

A lot of players prefer to eat pretty much the same meal or at least have one part of the meal--some players will even have an ice cream sundae--every night before the game. This is something that worked once and now is a staple in their meal. The main focus is to eat as if the food you're putting in your body serves as the fuel for a great morning and start to the day. Try not to drink any caffeine after 7pm as this will affect your sleep.

<u>10 pm The night before the game</u>

Next you need to catch some Z's. Think back to your previous games. Was the night before a deep sleep or a restless one? I'm not talking about the sleeping conditions-we all know road trips provide some tough beds, including greyhound bus seats-but what were the thoughts running through your head? Were they about the game? And were they negative or positive? Did anything keep you up? Based on sleep research you will want to sleep in 90 minute blocks. This means that if you are taking a nap it's good to rest either 1 ½ hours or 3 hours. At night this will translate to either 6 hours or 7 ½ hours of sleep.

This is pretty basic. I trust that you're not an insomniac zombie. However, I would like to deal with the thoughts going on upstairs before you fall asleep. I know from personal experience that sometimes I would lay awake for hours going over every detail of what could happen in tomorrow's game, including negative scenarios. With each thought, I would get more and more worked up so that my heart was basically beating through my chest. My mental state was going to crap as I looked over at the clock every half hour. You know the thoughts. They go something like this. If I go to sleep now I can get 5 hours of sleep. If I go to sleep right now I can get 4 hours and 10 minutes of sleep. After each group of thoughts I would look at the clock and realize time was ticking away. This resulted in my mind being frazzled and my body not being able to repair itself through a sufficient amount of rest.

You can help deal with this by using the relaxation techniques learned in the breathing section and visualization section. Find a few relaxing songs that will play for about 15-20 minutes. Quickly play a couple mind movies of you scoring, making a good defensive play, and ultimately leading your team to a win. This should put you in a good mood and allow your mind to temporarily forget about the game tomorrow night. Then practice the <u>Low Breathing</u> technique to relax your whole body. At this point in the night your body will be

ready to go to sleep based on your biorhythmic schedule, so just laying your head on the pillow will shut the door. Nighty Night, Jimmy Kyte.

8:00 – 9:00 am Wakeup Game day

When waking up it's crucial to get fluids into your body. Have a glass of water by your bed so you can crush it right when you wake up. Then grab some breakfast that provides you with the needed energy and hydration for the morning skate. If you don't have a morning skate then this will provide the baseline energy for any morning activities and get your day started right.

Not many people can jump right out of bed and get after it. A part of waking up is dealing with the grogginess. When you wake up make sure to roll over on the same side of the bed every time. ***(Just kidding.)*** **When you first wake up it's hard for your brain to handle complex thought processes. Any detailed mental activity will be wasted at this point. Some pros like to get the blood flowing with a quick walk before breakfast. If you do coffee or tea then walk to the nearest Starbucks instead of driving.**

8:30 - 10:00 am Breakfast

As you learned in the nutrition chapter, breakfast is the most important meal of the day. Thinking back, did you skip breakfast or grab something on the run? Maybe a nice sugary pop-tart or a Rice Krispie bar. I can't blame you for the easy fix in the morning because I rocked these a lot too, but you know as well as I do that it's not a great game day decision. As I said before our strength trainer in college used to monitor the dining hall access cards to see if everyone went to breakfast. It didn't matter if your first class was in the afternoon; you had a date over for a late night movie, or even closed the local watering hole. If you missed breakfast then you would pay dearly in the weight room. Skip this meal and you will be playing catch-up all day in order to get the needed energy for the night's game.

You need to get your lazy butt out of bed and eat

something of nutritional value. Pro teams on the road will have a spread of eggs, bacon, hash browns, etc. Don't eat too much or a lot of fat which will leave you feeling lethargic most of the morning and into the afternoon. There's not much routine here other than knowing the right foods to eat and getting properly hydrated. Many pros will grab a cup of coffee or tea to clear their head. You will find the correct amount of food to consume and the right foods by simple trial and error. Keep a journal of what you ate and your energy levels for the next 5 games. (This is something so small and easy but very important in order to find the right foods that work for you.) Mix and match different combinations so you can take what works and throw away what doesn't. Everybody is different.

10:30 - 11:30 am Pre-game Skate/Warm-up

The morning skate is usually a game day staple at the higher levels. If you don't have the option of a morning skate and are playing a night game, consider a bike ride or some other form of mild exercise. Did you have a morning skate or another exercise ritual to get the blow flowing in the morning? Did you begin to really think about the game at this point in the day?

Many of the pros' routines begin after the morning skate. A lot of players stay on the ice after practice for a quick game of rebound or practice shooting pucks. If you're a defenseman, try a few one timers on D-to-D cross ice passes at the blue line. If you're a forward take some passes in the slot for quick releases. If you're on the point for the power play, take some passes from the side boards. A forward can pile up a certain amount of pucks around the crease and practice going top shelf. Always end on a goal. Think back to the 80/20 rule you read before. Practice your strengths for maximum effectiveness in the upcoming game.

12:00 – 2:00 pm Time for yourself before the Pre-game Meal

The next step in the process is a 2 hour "layover" before the pre-game meal. I call it a layover because it's really a personal decision how you pass the hours. If your game time is different, then this can correspond to any free time you have during the day. When thinking back to prior game days, did you spend this time productively or did you simply watch T.V.? Did you spend much/any time thinking about the game? After getting a morning skate and feeling the jump in your legs did you have negative thoughts about your energy level and ability to perform that night? Were you worried about the rink conditions, fans, a nagging injury, or any other negative situation? This downtime can be used constructively to your mental advantage or it can destroy your confidence leading up to the game.

The "layover" is a great time to focus on your visualization and relaxation techniques learned in the previous chapters. You can go through an expanded breathing pattern and also use an extended visualization sequence. Everyone is different but it seems most beneficial to lie down in a quiet place to go through the above techniques. If your roommate has the TV on, then pop on the iPod and listen to some of your favorite relaxing music. For many of you this may be a new addition to your routine, but it's truly what separates the pros from those that never make it. You should have tried the basic techniques in the previous chapters on both breathing and visualization. Don't worry if it didn't come to you naturally or you had a hard time visualizing. It's something new that once worked into the routine and regularly practiced, will come easily. Soon you will begin to feel a quiet intensity as you lay there in your bed instead of wasting time watching TV or jabbering away. I guarantee this will positively change the way you play the game.

2:30 - 3:30 pm Pre-game Meal

The pre-game meal provides the added boost of energy

needed for the game. This is absolutely crucial to your legs either feeling light and quick, or heavy and dead. **(Everyday nutrition is the main factor of overall energy though. One meal isn't a quick fix for sloppy eating throughout the week.)** What did you eat before your last game? How many hours before the game did you eat? What did you drink before the game? How many portions did you consume? The optimal pre-game meal has been argued since Babe Ruth used to fuel up on hot dogs and beer, but the importance of it has become even more significant as everyone strives for an edge going into the game.

Many pros habitually eat the same things for every pre-game meal. If there's a game that night then they eat x, y, and z. It may be a precooked meal by yourself, a sit down meal prepared by your wife/girlfriend/parents, or if you're lucky and play for the New York Rangers it's a hole in the wall Italian joint that serves up the goods. That's the home game fare. The road game meals are almost always the same. "Chicken or Chicken" with a heap of pasta for carbs. Either way, it must be something that you regularly eat. Don't go trying lamb curry stew because you read about some marathon runner from Kenya who can run 100 miles through the lion infested grasslands without getting tired. Your stomach isn't conditioned to the new food and not only will your energy be affected but it may cause a few unwanted trips to the bathroom. You all know how hard that is when suited up.

If you need ideas, refer back to the nutrition chapter for what and how much to eat. These are only suggestions. It's better to realize the nutritional value of what you prefer to eat and incorporate these foods into your pre-game meal. As I said before, it's absolutely critical to keep a journal of what foods you ate and your subsequent energy levels (use a 1 to 5 scale to record your energy level). Also make sure you're getting the right amount of fluids to stay hydrated through your pre-game nap.

2:30 - 4:00 pm Pre-game Nap

After loading up at the pre-game meal, there's a period of time designated for a pre-game nap. I realize that youth hockey games are at sporadic times and can be either in the morning or afternoon, where catching a few zzz's isn't feasible. In these situations it's important to get a good sleep the night before in the case of morning games or a period of rest in the late morning for afternoon games. Kick your feet up and let your legs rest. It's not only the physical nature of the rest you get while napping, but also the mental aspect of it too. As I have mentioned before and what you clearly know is that hockey is a very stressful sport. Sitting up awake for two hours before the game in a stressful state will take its toll on the mind. The mental focus just won't be there without a period of rest before the game and the nap seems to rejuvenate your mind maybe more so than your legs. As talked about before, it's best to sleep in periods of 90 minute intervals. Set your alarm for 1 hour and 35 to 40 minutes from the time you lay down, which will give you a few minutes to fall asleep and the optimal sleeping time.

As you think back to prior game days, did your routine take this into account? What did you do about 4 hours before the game? Were you running around doing things completely unrelated to the game? Hanging out with your friends? Playing a little mini hockey? Think back to when you had your best legs. (When your legs were light and quick as you were flying around the ice.) What did you do over the course of that day? Now think back to when your legs felt as heavy as lead. (Like you were skating around in quicksand.) What did you do differently during the course of this day compared to the prior game day when you felt great? It could be a combination of your nutrition, hydration and mental focus. But your overall energy level relies on the recharging of both your physical and mental battery to play your best.

Most pro players I know have incorporated the nap into their game day routine. The first year when the schedule calls for a pre-game nap is beautiful. At first you don't want

to feel groggy due to a nap before the big game. Your nerves are hard to quiet down, but then you start doing it and it's the best sleep of your life. You wake up feeling refreshed and ready to go. Before the nap it's best to forget about the game. Play a relaxing tune on your iPod and shut 'er down.

<u>**4:30 - 6:00 pm Arrive at the Rink**</u>

Now it's time to move forward into game mode. Your mind should begin to tune everything out but the game. This step is where many players have complicated routines that are very specific. It allows them to first eliminate distractions and then put all focus on the present. Nothing else matters for the next 5 hours other than the game, your performance, and winning. Everything else is a distraction pulling your focus away.

Did you have a specific routine that you went through when you got to the rink? Do you put your equipment on the same way or tape your stick the same before every game? Do you do something before every game that helps you prepare? If your routine gets interrupted, does it become a distraction and mess with your mental preparation?

Many pro players have a different individual way of getting pumped up for the game. If you notice a player's on-ice demeanor, there's a good chance you will get a sense of his pre-game attitude. Paul Kariya was as serious as a heart attack and his old teammate Teemu Selanne was light and loose. It's all a matter of the player's personality and what worked in the past. Hank Aaron said the most important thing is how a person prepares to do battle. Bo Jackson, considered one of the greatest athletes of all time, would make up an alter ego that he compared to Jason from the Friday the 13th movies. He said "I refused to let him out of his box, except on Sundays in the fall when I strapped on my helmet to play football." However, no matter what type of attitude players display before the game, they get to their peak state or "the zone" with routines. Below are a few steps in a pro's routine that you can incorporate into your own

game. You may recognize or even already use some of these routines and others will be completely new to you. Just as before with the other suggestions, try them and choose what works best for you.

1. **Do individual stretches away from the team.**
2. **Tape all your sticks the same way before every game.**
3. **Put all your equipment on in the same order. (Gretzky preaches this in the *Wayne Gretzky: Hockey My Way* video.)**
4. **Stone/sharpen your skates.**
5. **Clean you Itech Shield.**
6. **Tape your fingers or wrists.**
7. **Tape your shin pads the same way.**
8. **Run the stairs.**
9. **Grab a couple of guys and play one of the warm up games from the earlier chapter.**
10. **Bike for 5-10 minutes.**
11. **Stickhandle in the hallway or on the empty ice.**
12. **Grab another guy and pass the puck/ball back and forth for a few minutes.**
13. **Use a Visualization or Breathing technique.**
14. **Play a couple of pump up tunes on the iPod.**
15. **Grab Water or Gatorade to drink (make sure to stay hydrated).**
16. **Have a quick snack from the nutritional chapter.**

Many players use a combination of the above steps to get themselves ready for every game. By the time most players reach the pro level they have internalized an individually specific routine. It's become as familiar as lacing up their skates.

7:00 -7:20 pm Right before the game

Have you noticed that right before the game, you hit an emotional peak whether good or bad? If you're prone to overanalyzing everything, then your nerves may get the best of you before the game even begins. Did you think of "What if" scenarios concerning negative plays and outcomes? Or did you have thoughts of failure or incompetence, such as, do I measure up to the players in the other dressing room? Almost everyone has had these thoughts at some point, but many young and inexperienced players have these thoughts nearly every game. I had them myself. *THESE ARE TOTALLY USELESS THOUGHTS THAT WE'RE GOING TO ELIMINATE WITH A SET ROUTINE.* Your coach, teammates, friends and family know you're good enough to play at this level. You wouldn't be there if you didn't deserve it. Now it's up to you to play your best. By now the analytical part of your mind should be shut off. You need to trust your skills that you've worked so hard to hone over the course of the season. If your entire pre-game runs smoothly up until game time then you have thoughts of doubt or get nervous it's all been wasted. You need specific thoughts to get you into the relaxed concentrated "zone" as referred to earlier in the book. What do the pros do that sets them apart at this crucial stage on game day?

It's interesting to see a camera shot of an NHL team in the locker room before a game. There's not much talking- other than the pump up nonsense that some of the vocal players throw out. Players are staring blankly ahead or down at the ground, lost in their thoughts. Depending on the player and his role in the game, these thoughts can be anything from game time assignments, defensive schemes, prior well-played games, scoring the big goal tonight, etc. It's the one time where many players consistently use quick visualization sequences to push themselves into the right mind state for game time success. This includes the 10 quick mind movies developed in the visualization chapter. This puts you in a positive state leading up until you step on the ice.

7:30-10:00 pm During the Game

As a player growing up, the period would end and a minute would be placed on the clock. Not much time to think about anything other than what the coach is drawing up on the dry erase. As you get older and continue to play at higher levels, you come to the point where the fans get a bathroom/beer run break and you get 15 minutes to think over all the positive/negative things that happened during the prior period. This can be good and bad. If you do have a break between periods did you hydrate yourself? Did you dwell on mistakes? Did you think about making them again in the next period or learn from them and forget about them going forward? It's been said that the greatest players have the shortest memory.

Everybody knows the power of momentum. I'm sure you've all witnessed its game changing power first hand. This is the hardest force to stop, even for pro players. The ice seems tilted, and the players start to either believe completely in themselves or on the other hand doubt themselves. Every period ends with a certain team gaining momentum to the other team's detriment, no matter how small. I believe at this point in the game a player's attitude can be as contagious as a virus. Once the game begins there will be ups and downs but you should always be in the moment. However, between periods when you have time to think, your mind may drift back to a mistake made earlier in the game. Many players have a routine between periods to either pump themselves up to reach a higher level or maintain the optimal state they are already playing.

The mistakes have been made and are going to show up on the video tape session tomorrow whether you continue to think about them or quickly forget them. Simply take the lesson from your mistake and then toss it. If you make the necessary adjustment next period, then you will automatically be better in that area. The pros know this. Listen to an interview between periods. A player starts by stating what they could do better to counteract what the

other team is doing. Then they talk about doing it. They're always looking forward and staying positive. The best way to forget about mistakes and control your thoughts is to do something to take your mind off of whatever may be bothering you. Go back to any of the possible routines before the game that eliminated distractions. Some simply ways pros stay focused in the present include:

1. **Re-taping their sticks**
2. **Taking off half or even all of their equipment like Bernie Nichols.**
3. **Grabbing a couple of cups of Gatorade.**
4. **Taking off your skates or at least untying them to give your feet a rest.**
5. **Talking to your line-mates about opportunities that you can take advantage of next period.**

The most important thing to remember is that next period is a new start. Momentum is hard to keep over a 15-minute break- good or bad. Of course learn from your mistakes but keep it positive. No matter what the obstacle you may face on the scoreboard, just know that there's a team in the past that has overcome it. Play your game and stay positive.

9:30-10:00 pm Post Game

After the game many young and inexperienced players just get dressed and go home. Pros realize that after a hard game, the body needs a form of light exercise for a cool down period to flush out the lactic acid. As you walk out of the locker room the physical and mental stress as well as the final score will weigh heavily on you. It's always important to remember that hockey is a marathon not a short sprint. You need to keep a positive mental attitude no matter the outcome of the game. Also due to the nature of the sport you most likely have some bumps and bruises that need attention in order to keep yourself in the best possible health for the next games. Do you have a post game routine? Do you take a bad game away from the rink?

Pros know that the season is long and although each

game is important in the standings, you must be able to maintain the focus and keep an upbeat attitude required to play your best night in/night out. This requires mental and physical housekeeping every post game. The results of your individual performance will weigh on you- good or bad. Just as between the periods, you must learn from mistakes and quickly forget them. From a coaching standpoint, you might be reminded of this again in the video session but you have to remember not to take it personally. It's a learning tool to make you better. The key is to take away the positives from the game. This can be done by talking through good defensive and offensive plays with your line mates or parents. If it's a tough loss and the room is silent, go over positive plays in your mind and build off them. This game is over, but there are many more to go. Physically the body needs to recover from the beating you took (or hopefully gave) out on the ice. A good post game routine will help your body repair muscle damage, fill up the body's fuel tanks, replenish fluid levels, and help re-energize you from fatigue. Think of the time between games as a process you follow that has several parts. Following physical exertion, you enjoy a 30-minute window of opportunity when the muscles are ready to take up energy from food sources. So immediately after the game, have a high density carbohydrate based fluid available for consumption (i.e. gatorade) along with a carbohydrate-protein mixed food source (i.e. turkey sandwich). This fast tracks energy refueling and has a big impact on the next day's workout/practice/game.

Post-game, while your muscles are warm and more elastic, use static stretching to help flush out the lactic acid from the legs, increase the length of muscles, and tune up the body by spending more time on tighter muscles. Post-game (and post-practice) players are mentally and physically tired but the stretching program needs to become a habit that is done consistently.

In order to succeed in hockey you need to put your body on the line. Over a long season this will take its toll. I advise you to get into the habit of following a specific routine, choosing a mix of methods that help recovery during particularly fatigued states.

Summary of the Routine Chapter

- Every athlete has his/her own routine, whether consciously or unconsciously, that puts them in game state.
- Routines eliminate distractions, narrow focus for the game, keep a player emotionally stable no matter how important the game, and also help the player "shut off" his brain to the negative thoughts/doubts he may have concerning the upcoming game.
- Don't get caught up in your routine.
- The routine you adapt and use will be the same every game.

For a night game, players have different routines at set times leading up to the game. Your routine may be completely different than any other player but *consider doing something at these time intervals to get your mind in game mode.*

7:30 pm The night before the game

- What you eat and drink is critical for a good night's sleep and energy in the morning.

10 pm The night before the game

- Get a good 6 to 7 ½ hours of sleep.
- Use a breathing or visualization technique to relax and think positive thoughts before conking out.

8:00 – 9:00 am Wakeup Game day

- Grab a glass of water immediately upon waking.

8:30-10:00 am Breakfast

- Eat a light nutritious breakfast for energy during the morning skate.

10:30 to 11:30 am Pre-game Skate/Warm-up

- Stick around after practice to shoot pucks or stretch. Use the 80/20 technique from the visualization section to focus on specific situations that you are going to face in tonight's game. Begin to get mentally prepared for the game.

12:00 – 2:00 pm Time to Yourself before the Pre-game Meal

- Use the breathing techniques to get into a relaxed state.
- Use the extended visualization technique (mind movies) to get mentally ready for the game.
- Listen to relaxing music (whatever you choose).

2:30 to 3:30 pm Pre-game Meal

- From your journal, you should know what foods are best for you. Eat these foods.
- Focus on low glycemic carbohydrates.
- Make sure to hydrate.
- Get a lean source of protein into your body.

2:30 -4:00 pm Pre-game Nap

- If possible get 90 minutes of sleep for proper mental and physical rest before the game.

4:30 -5:15 pm Arrive at the Rink

- Tune everything out but the game ahead.
- Every pro has a different routine. Use your current routine and incorporate some from the list to develop a set routine.

7:00 -7:20pm Right before the Game

- Experiment with using a quick visualization sequence for positive thoughts---10 quick mind movies---
- Shut off your thinking mind and trust your skills.
- Stay hydrated and grab a quick medium- to- high glycemic snack

7:30-10:00 pm During the Game

- Stay hydrated.
- Quickly learn from mistakes then forget them.
- Use breathing techniques to counteract stress.
- Develop a routine to keep yourself in the present moment between periods when your mind can drift or your thinking about mistakes in the previous periods.

9:30-10:00 pm Post Game

- Replace lost fluids

- Perform a light exercise and use static stretches to remove lactic acid.
- Get a good meal into your system to replenish you energy for tomorrow's game
- Take care of any bumps and bruises.

Top 8 Mistakes Amateurs Make

1. **Trying an exercise or drill 1 time and then giving up and proclaiming that it doesn't work.** A lot of the drills and exercises in this book are completely new to you. You can and will see immediate results with most of the exercises outlined in the book. However, in order to really take your game to the highest level you will need to continually practice them. The more familiar and comfortable you become with a technique, the more it will translate onto the ice.

2. **Worrying about what other people think.** This is a big one. Hockey players have a tendency to get after one another. Or in other words, they will find a weakness and mercifully chirp you until they see a crack. It's not that they're trying to be mean. They expect the same in return. It's just a weird way to pass the time with your friends on long bus trips. But anyway, if you start something like the techniques in this book that are foreign to most people, expect to hear some ribbing. Don't let this stop you. If you let other people control your pre-game routine, you're essentially letting other people dictate your mental attitude come game time.

3. **Trying to incorporate all of the drills and exercises in this book at the same time.** There are over 100 specific exercises in this book, including stretches. Trying to remember and optimally use each one before tonight's game simply isn't realistic. Hopefully you tried all the drills and exercises as you read through the chapters. There were some techniques and exercises that jumped out at you and you know without a doubt can help your game. Reread that portion of the book and try those for the next week. Take what works and toss what doesn't. Then do

the same with 5 other drills or exercises that you know will help. Keep building and building your knowledge base. Pretty soon you will find yourself better prepared going into each game and really see results.

4. **Getting too caught up mentally in one specific exercise or drill such as a long complicated routine. "Essentially putting all your eggs in one basket."** The book outlines 7 different areas that you can use to improve your overall hockey game with a narrow focus on pre-game preparation. And there are many more. If you only rely on one exercise, you first won't benefit from the other options and secondly it has a high potential to become a mental crutch.

5. **Not analyzing your game with the 80/20 approach-explained in a visualization chapter-to pinpoint your strengths.** Everyone reading this plays a different individual game. Take a step back and analyze your past games, including successes and failures. What are you great at? What do you need work on? You may have a hard shot but are physically small. It only makes sense then to spend a majority of your individual practice time getting open in the slot and working on a quick release. You can still spend some time thinking about and working on battling a defenseman for rebound position, but it's not going to make the same positive difference on the ice.

6. **Striving for endless perfection.** Hockey is highly competitive. Everyone playing the game is striving to get better. (Some more than others.) On the ice and off you want to be the best. That's the only attitude I would expect from a hockey player, especially someone reading this book. This however is a lot different then seeking perfection. *It's not attainable.* You're going to make

mistakes. And you're going to make them every game. If you're really honest with yourself you make them every shift. No big deal. It's a teaching tool. If you beat yourself up thinking about every past mistake then it's impossible to move forward. The exercises from the book will help you cut down on errors not eliminate them. And when you do make an error-no matter how big-the exercises and drills in this book will help you forget it.

7. **Viewing tonight's game as the "be all end all" of your entire hockey playing career.** Hockey is a long season. Of course every game is very important. 2 points early in the season can mean making the playoffs 6 months later. That's not what I'm getting at. Remember, you must find the right pre-game attitude that's right for you, that gets the best results day-in-day-out. Then hold on to that no matter if it's the preseason or postseason. Yeah, some games the pressure is turned up, but internalizing that doesn't help you or the team.

8. **Ignoring the fun you have off the ice with your teammates and parents. Ignoring the interesting places you get to see while traveling for hockey. Ignoring the experiences.** For me there was always another season, another game, and another shift. Until, because of an injury, there wasn't. That injury occurred almost 8 years ago. I miss playing the game so much, but when I look back all I can see are the friends I made in hundreds of locker rooms and bus rides. I remember the trips to Europe for hockey tournaments with Team USA. I remember the collective team feeling of big wins and big losses. I remember getting up at 6 a.m. for workout sessions with my team. And so much more. But unless I really concentrate on specific games, it's hard to remember on-ice situations. The behind the scenes fun and

friendships made has already overshadowed the actual game. I'm now 29 years old. I'm broke because I spend all my money visiting hockey friends in life celebrations such as weddings, bachelor parties, and the birth of their kids. Because of my injury I can only get on the ice a couple of times a year, but sitting in that locker room before and after the game you have a group of instant friends. You meet the greatest people in the game of hockey and get to see some interesting places too. My life has literally been shaped by hockey and I'm grateful for it. As Ferris says in the movie Ferris Bueller's Day Off "Life moves pretty fast. You don't stop and look around once in a while, you could miss it."

Ending Chapter

I would like to end the book with an excerpt from Mark Messier's retirement speech that you can read and reread whenever you find yourself stressed out or overwhelmed during the season.

"And I would just like to end by saying, a quote that I took from Mike Richter in an article that he had done lately. If I can just quickly read it to you, if I can see it. *(He has been crying for almost the entire length of his 15 minute speech.)* He said, "In sports, in its best light is about challenging yourself and improving you as a person. It's not about looking for a medal at the end of an event. It's about a journey in which your physical and mental well-being improves through physical activity." And unfortunately in pro sports we sometimes get derailed into the ultimate goal of winning a Stanley Cup, but I wanted to read that because for all of us who have children that are in minor hockey, it's not about becoming a professional athlete, it's about the journey and the people you meet along the way. And the life lessons that you get from playing an incredible game. Thank you."[17]

And Thank you. I hope that you put the 7 steps of pro preparation to use to further enhance your enjoyment of the greatest sport on earth.

[17] http://www.hhof.com/LegendsOfHockey/html/indspeeches.htm

Acknowledgements

First, I must thank my writer friend Pete who initially gave me the idea for this book while traveling up the Australian coast chasing good times.

To my brother Garrett (who took the front cover picture) and my sister Marissa who proofread the copies and always offered encouragement I thank you. Without your positive support I wouldn't have finished the first draft.

My old roommates Lendo, Reeder, and Reeder's gf Farris who helped everyway they could and bared with me when I got particularly rattled. I spent more time staring blankly into a computer screen then cleaning the place for a couple of years. Taco Tuesdays should be on me for the next year.

My Grandpa Friess who thought I could do anything including changing my own oil. I wish you were around to read the final copy. I always enjoyed spending the time I got to see you and Grandma Friess in Estevan, Sask.

To my Uncle Colin and his entire family for pushing any of my ideas on his buddies and teams in the Great White North.

To my Uncle Alan who has helped me think through a lot of my ideas and has a great many himself.

To my beautiful girlfriend Meghan who edited the entire book. Taking my thoughts and helping me organize them into a finished book was a Herculean task. Without you I would still be editing all the green underlined sentences in Microsoft Word.

My parents, Lorne and Cathye Henning, who have encouraged me every step of the way. I'm sure you think most of the ideas and plans I run by you are a little crazy but if there's any light at the end of the tunnel you push me forward into it.

Last but not least, this book is dedicated to Grandpa Henning. I will always remember playing hockey on the pond in Minnesota for hours on end. I'm pretty sure no one has as much patience as you. And I know that no one watches more hockey. Thanks for passing on that love for the game. I wish Grandma could put this down next to her Reader's Digest collection after reading it.

About the Author

Brett Henning, former collegiate hockey player and member of the 2000 U.S.A World Junior Team, currently lives in Orange County, CA. After getting injured his junior year and told that his back could crumble like a coffee cake, he traveled to Australia for 10 months. His love of travel has put him on many planes, trains, and automobiles where a book in hand is crucial. As an avid reader, he stumbled upon the self-help category of books and wanted to translate this information into a useful hockey reference for all players young and old. This is his first book. Due to his injury and a subsequent surgery, he can no longer play hockey but currently trains players at Athletic Republic in Orange County, CA. His surfing career was over before it even started.

Also Available from Score100goals

This is a unique shooter tutor that teachers players where to shoot from 5 different mapped out areas in the offensive zone. Goalies are taught to play the angles from the first time they strap on the pads. **How come goal scorers are not? And why have we been aiming at the same 5 holes for the past 25 years?** Goalies have completely changed their style to the butterfly. After analyzing over a 1,000 NHL goals a number of scoring patterns emerged. From this I was able to divide the offensive zone into 5 areas. From these 5 areas I was able to plot the specific targets on the net where the most goals were scored. This gives you the best probability to score from different angles and distance within the offensive zone. The zones and target areas are color coordinated to speed up the learning process. **Practice on the Score100goals Shooter Tutor and you will have the quickest release on your team. It teaches a goal scorers instinct so you know where to shoot for the best probability of scoring without even looking at the goal.**

Available at Score100goals.com

For a complete breakdown of the 5 zones and where to shoot, visit the same site.

Also Available from Score100goals

Hockey Sniper

An *iPhone/itouch App* that further familiarizes hockey players with where to shoot for the best probability of scoring from different angles and distances to the net in the offensive zone. Using the Score100goals shooter tutor from above, the practice mode walks you through where to shoot. Then "Game Time" mode has progressively harder levels so you must master where to shoot in the blink of the eye. Nothing will replace the sweat and blistered hands you get from shooting 100's of pucks in the driveway-especially on the Score100goals shooter tutor-but this game will beat those zones and where to shoot into your head.

Available for your iPhone and iPod touch at the App Store. The name of the app is Hockey Sniper. The url is www.itunes.com/app/hockeysniper

Sign up for the Score100goals Newsletter at:

www.score100goals.com/newsletter.html

Receive weekly information on skills to practice, unique ways of looking at the game, tips, and other cool writings and videos.